IT IS WELL.

IT IS WELL!

by
Shana Wilson Anderson

Copyright © 2020 by Shana Wilson Anderson
ISBN: 13: 978-1537332369
ISBN-10: 1537332368

Unless otherwise indicated,
all Scripture quotations are taken from
the *King James Version* of the Bible.

It Is Well!
ISBN-13: 978-1537332369
Copyright © 2020 by Shana Wilson Anderson
shanawilsonanderson@gmail.com

Published by CreateSpace Independent Publishing Platform

Printed in the United States of America.
All rights reserved under International Copyright Law.
Content and/or cover may not be reproduced in whole or in part without the express written permission of the Publisher, except for the use of brief quotations in a book review.

Dedication

First, I give honor to my Lord and Savior who instructed and guided me to write this book. I pray that every word is a word from the Lord. I dedicate this book to every mother and wife who is lost and lonely and struggling to save her family. I dedicate this book to my sons, DeShawn and DeAndre Anderson. Thank you for being perfect in your imperfections. I am proud to be your mother. Lastly, to my husband and best friend Chad, thank you for your unconditional love and support. I am who I am because of my family.

Love

Shana

Table of Contents

Introduction

Chapter 1 – The Preparation	1
Chapter 2 – Your Relationship: Rise Up	8
Chapter 3 – What Have You Asked Him for Lately?	24
Chapter 4 – I Surrender All	32
Chapter 5 – Let Us Pray	39
Chapter 6 – Fasting	48
Chapter 7 – Promises of God	60
Chapter 8 – The Wait	65
Chapter 9 – The Attack	73
Chapter 10 – The Process	88
Chapter 11 – The Test	94
Chapter 12 – The Anointing	101
Chapter 13 – Break Every Chain	109
Chapter 14 – Power	116
Chapter 15 – The Turnaround	123
Chapter 16 – Praise and Worship	131
Chapter 17 – Miracles, Signs and Wonders	138
Chapter 18 – It Is Well!	143

Acknowledgements

Biography

Introduction

It began as a scene from a bad dream. I felt trapped, with no place to hide and no one to call for help. I jumped in my car and drove frantically, no particular destination in mind. After driving several miles, I finally pulled over on the side of the road, exhausted and crying hysterically, yelling at God, "Why me? I am a good person. I go to church and try to live right." Grabbing my cell phone, I wondered, "Who should I call?" I needed to talk to someone to help calm me down. But who? I couldn't call my sister, because she wouldn't understand. My best friend had her own problems, so I didn't want to bother her. If I called my mom, she would worry and I definitely didn't want that.

My mind ran from one person to the next and no one came to mind that I could actually call. With everything I had going on I wanted—no needed—someone who could and would understand. My life felt like it was in shambles. I heard a voice say I should just kill myself and it would all be over. I even stopped to consider how I would do it. I knew my gun was within reach, under the arm rest. I also knew I didn't have the nerve to take my own life. I placed the phone in the passenger seat and wept for what seemed like hours. In desperation I cried out, "Lord, please help me. I need you!"

In that instance, an indescribable feeling of peace washed over me. I could smell a sweet, pleasant aroma and I felt as if someone had just wrapped me in the warmest, most comforting embrace. I looked around, but I was still alone in the car. It was time to get back to reality. My mini melt down was over. I stopped crying, grabbed my phone and entered my address into the GPS. It was time for me to find my way. I needed an outlet to release all my feelings and frustrations. I needed a place of peace. That night I decided my life would benefit from a GPS of its own. It was time for me to find my way.

I longed to have a relationship with someone who would encourage, guide and support me. I had a void that needed to be filled. I had always struggled with sharing myself completely with others. I didn't want people judging me. On the surface, I had the perfect life. Married to my high school boyfriend, two smart and handsome kids, nice house, nice cars, great career... It was the American dream, right? All those things and still something was missing. I didn't realize it at the time but what I was truly longing for was a relationship with God.

I discovered an outlet that allowed me to be free and to release some stress whenever I felt the need. I began to journal my thoughts and my feelings. I wrote every chance I could. I wrote when I was happy; I wrote when I was sad. If I was in church, I wrote my interpretation of the message. I constantly read my Bible and enjoyed watching sermons on cable and took note on key points that felt relevant to what I was going through at the time. When difficult situations arose, I was able to freely express my emotions without the fear of being judged. Keeping a journal provided an awesome way to release my thoughts in a safe, judgment-free private venue. It was where I received my healing. As I reviewed my writings, I could see God's presence in every aspect of my life. The more I wrote I felt something special stirring inside me. A simple practice begun years ago remains a part of my life even until this day.

God continued to talk to me throughout the years and I continued to write. Yes, I said talk to me. For several years, I could not hear in the natural but He still communicated to me.

He is talking to you also; you may not have realized it yet. Sometimes, He speaks to me through a song. At others, in casual conversation, I hear the answer to a question previously asked.

There have been several instances when God has woken me up in the middle of the night and given me specific scriptures to read. This blows my mind every time it happens. During this season, I was reading about the Apostle Paul. I was not certain why I was reading it but continued to read it over and over.

One Monday afternoon, I decided to go to noon day services. Of course, where else would I be on a Monday. It was part of my weekly routine. The service was uplifting and motivating. Then there was an interesting chain of events that occurred. The minister of the services called for everyone to gather in a circle to close with prayer. We quickly began to stack all of the chairs against the wall so we could form a huge circle in the center of the building. There was a young lady that came and stood next to me and held my hand as the minister closed in prayer. Then to my surprise, she began to appear to speak in tongues. I am not an interpreter so I assumed that's what she was doing. I felt uncomfortable and did not feel the warm presence of the Holy Spirit as I had earlier. The tighter she held my hand the more uncomfortable I became. I began to pray to block out her ramblings and noise. At the end of the prayer, she mumbled something about writing me a check for $100,000 and asked if I was in the marketing field. I replied no but I was hoping to start my own business. She then proceeded to tell me she was currently unemployed and suggested that we should talk later. She handed me her phone number and left the building. My friend who was observing our interaction came over and grabbed both of my hands and began to pray over me. His prayers were that God not allow any spirit to be transferred to me. I was confused on what had just occurred but still felt safe. As I was leaving the church, I noticed my stomach felt nauseous. I drove a few miles when all of a sudden I began to profusely sweat and my head ached as if it would explode. I knew something was wrong and quickly used my car's Bluetooth to dial my friend who had also just left the church service. I tried to explain what I was feeling and she stopped me mid-sentence and began to pray. For a few minutes, I was sick throwing up a white foamy substance and I was actually on top of a bridge. I pulled as far to the right as I could. After a few minutes, I felt better and continued my journey back to work. When I arrived at work, I was still pondering the situation that had just occurred. As I sat at my desk, the Holy Spirit told me I needed someone to pray over me again. I immediately sent an instant message to one of my co-workers, who I knew had a relationship with God, to meet me in one of the office's conference rooms. When she arrived, I quickly explained what happened and she also began to pray with me. For several minutes, I continued to purge the same white substance as before. This time I felt completely restored to my normal self. We began to talk and through our conversation she confirmed that my earlier situation was actually an attack due to my spiritual gift. Spiritual gift? I wasn't convinced but she definitely had my attention. She then started to talk about Paul. I was once again speechless. Why was the story of Paul constantly coming up?

I began to think about Paul and his purpose. I re-read the entire book of Acts and even went to my friend—the Internet—to search for a deeper understanding of Paul's purpose. I discovered Paul was an evangelist. The purpose of an evangelist is to spread the Word of God with the intention of saving lives. It took some time for me to understand God was giving me instructions for what He wanted me to do.

In Acts 18:9, the Lord spoke to Paul one night in a vision, "Do not be afraid; keep on speaking, do not be silent. For I am with you, and no one is going to attack and harm you, because I have many people in this city." When I questioned God about what I should do, I found the answer in His Word, Acts 22:10: "You will be told all things which are appointed for you to do." I submitted my life to God and began to trust Him. I knew I would face insults, rejection and some difficult trials, but I was excited because I understood my purpose. Like Paul, my instruction was to keep speaking. I have been called to tell my story. And this is my story.

How do you describe your relationship with God?

Thoughts:

_____
_____
_____
_____
_____
_____
_____
_____
_____
_____

So it was, when the man of God saw her afar off, that he said to his servant Gehazi, Look, the Shunammite woman! Please run now to meet her, and say to her, "Is it well with you? Is it well with your husband? Is it well with the child?" And she answered,

"It is well."

2 KINGS 4:25-4:26

Chapter 1 – The Preparation

"Why me?" Have you asked yourself this question a time or two? I am willing to guess the answer is, "Yes." Here is another question for you to consider: Why not you? You are amazing and perfect, even with all your imperfections and faults. When God created you, He created you with a specific purpose in mind. Romans 8:1 says, "*There is* therefore now no condemnation to those who are in Christ Jesus, who do not walk according to the flesh, but according to the Spirit. Therefore, the Lord looks beyond your faults and sees you as He intended. In every situation, He wants you to realize that when you need Him, He is still there—holding your hand, wiping your tears or merely pushing you forward. We often get stuck in the middle of our mess because we are so focused on our current situation that we forget to look to Him for direction. God Almighty gave you the power you need to overcome your situation. Yes, YOU! The instructions for tapping into your power are so simple, it will surprise you. I am getting ahead of myself. Let me start at the beginning.

In my early thirties, I started having a little interest or shall I say curiosity on religion and God. Like many of us, I went to church when I was young and was baptized. I knew of God but I did not know Him for myself. I rededicated myself at church and even purchased a one-a-day Bible that helped me organize into 365 daily readings from the Old and New Testament. Day after day, life moved on and my Bible collected dust on my nightstand. I realize now that my relationship with God really began to ignite when I started having knee problems. What began as morning stiffness, gradually increased to the point I could barely walk. The pain was unbearable at times. Like many others when we are down, our prayer life increases. I prayed to God to remove the pain and heal me. I went to a doctor who informed me that I needed to have knee surgery. Normally, I did not have a fear of hospitals or surgery but this time it was different. I was very nervous and could barely sleep the night before. The next morning, I arrived at the hospital and was quickly changed into my not so Victoria Secret's gown. My doctor came in and warmly greeted my husband, my mom and I. He began to say that he was just a vessel doing God's work and asked if he and his staff could pray with me prior to the anesthesiologist putting me to sleep. I gladly accepted. It was comforting to know my surgeon was a man of God. His prayer helped easy my fears regarding the surgery and the next thing I recall was waking up hours later to go home. It was tough the first few days. I mostly laid in bed and cried. My recovery time was expected to take about two months.

About midway through my recovery, I was lying in bed and I looked over on my nightstand and noticed my Bible where I had sat it after a few months of reading. I recalled a promise I had made to myself over nine months before to read the entire Bible before my 35th birthday. I looked at the date and realized I had less than three months to complete this task. I had better get busy or I would miss my deadline. During every free moment, I read my Bible. Did I understand it all? Of course not, but I continued reading. I was intrigued by what I had discovered while reading and hungered to know more. As I read the Bible, it read like a soap opera. The stories were fascinating and the desire within me increased to learn more about God. I continued until I had completed the entire Bible. And yes, I did it by my birthday. This was the most special present I have ever given myself.

God is merciful and such a gentleman. He did not rush me into a relationship with Him. He was patient with me. Little did I know God would use this season not only to prepare me for what was to come over the next several years, but also for the rest of my life. I seriously doubt I would have picked up my Bible again if I had not found myself with so much free time following my knee surgery.

It was the beginning of the best relationship I have ever known. I have found this to be THE relationship that can and will help you through any situation you may encounter. My goal is to share how God used my life experiences to usher me into the best relationship ever. Paul suffered beatings, near death experiences and imprisonment. But he reminds us in Romans 8:28, "that all things work together for good to those who love God and to those who are called according to His purpose." Every situation you have encountered was predestined by God. He either did it or allowed it. As you read through each chapter, I pray you will come to understand how your current situations are changing your relationship with Him.

Scripture Reading

Hebrew 13:20-21

Now may the God of peace, who through the blood of the eternal covenant brought back from the dead our Lord Jesus, that great Shepherd of the sheep, equip you with everything good for doing his will, and may he work in us what is pleasing to him, through Jesus Christ, to whom be glory for ever and ever. Amen.

Affirmation:

God created me with a specific purpose in mind. I will not worry if I haven't figured everything out yet. I will. Every situation that I will encounter is destined by God. He wants me to realize that He is always with me. And every situation is shaping me to become my unapologetic self.

Who am I? I describe myself as……

Thoughts:

_____

_____

_____

_____

Prayer:

Heavenly Father, as you prepare me, open my eyes and ears to your word. Father give me the knowledge and confidence to believe in myself. Increase my desire to read your word. Lord fill me up with your word so I can fulfill your word. Amen.

Chapter 2 – Your Relationship: Rise Up

As you begin this journey, you will create your own personal relationship with God. Yes, your very own relationship. No one has the same relationship and you should not compare yours to anyone.

I remember attending my first women's retreat. I was so excited about attending. Everyone at church had shared what a life-changing an awesome experience it had been for them during previous years and that it was a must-go-to event for every woman of God. I was like a kid on Christmas Eve. I was expecting something great to happen at the retreat. Earlier that week, I was in deep prayer. I was actually praying in my sleep. I awoke around midnight and couldn't recall exactly what I was praying for but I knew God was going to answer my prayers. I had been praying constantly about my children, my husband and my job so I am sure it was the same. I could feel His presence and I was comforted. I got up and went into the bathroom not to wake my husband. I knew I couldn't explain what was happening. I began to quietly shout and praise God and a feeling of joy overcame my body and I began to weep. The next morning I received a text message from my manager. She said I was on her mind and sent me two scriptures to read. The first was John 4:4-6, which reads, "You, dear children, are from God and have overcome them, because the one who is in you is greater than the one who is in the world. They are from the world and therefore speak from the viewpoint of the world, and the world listens to them. We are from God, and whoever knows God listens to us; but whoever is not from God does not listen to us. This is how we recognize the Spirit of truth and the spirit of falsehood." And the second was Genesis 12:2, "I will make you into a great nation, and I will bless you; I will make your name great, and you will be a blessing." As I read the scriptures, I couldn't help to wonder if God was speaking to me. Was he actually saying that he was blessing me and he wants me to continue to spread His word? Because of my obedience He will answer my prayers. I continued to pray that He would be a guiding light in our lives. I asked Him to watch over our every step and word. And I thanked him for giving me so much time alone so that I could truly hear from Him. I did not know what to expect next but I knew it would be awesome. I speculated that we would all be gathered in the room praying and God would appear before and leave us with a deep profound message or he would show us a glimpse of our futures. My imagination was running wild and needless to say God did leave us with a deep profound message and he did leave us with hopes about our futures.

The theme of for the weekend was *Women at the Well Thirsting for a Drink of the Living Water*. I had no clue what that meant, but I sure wanted a taste.

The speaker's message was clear and she explained it perfectly: "As women, we look at things and people to fulfill a need in our life but nothing seems to satisfy the thirst we have but God. Do you feel empty? Is there something missing that you can't quite put your hands on? Have you maxed out your credit cards shopping trying to find happiness? Have you dated your share of men and there is still that burning desire because something seems to still be missing from your life? Are you married but feel your relationship could be better? I am here to tell you that you are drinking the wrong kind of water. You need to learn to depend on God not another man or thing to fill you need. Lean on Him until your cup runneth over. But to do this you must go through a process first."

I was so excited because she was talking to me, about me. At the end of service, she asked that anyone who wanted a closer relationship with God to come to the altar for prayer. I jumped at the chance to give God praise and to ask him to fill my cup. As we stood there praying and praising God, the preacher rested her hands on me and I literally fell to the floor. I was laid out by the Holy Spirit. I could hear God clearly say, "Shana, I hear you. Let it go." So I did. I had prayed all week and expected something big to happen and God showed up in a mighty way. That night I returned to my room excited about what God was doing in my life. I grabbed my pen and wrote down as much as I could recall about the evening. The last sentence I wrote said, "I am so unworthy but God continues to have favor in my life." After that, I went to sleep, and for the first time in a while, I truly got a good night of rest.

I was excited and thought God had already done what He was going to do for me on the retreat. Little did I know I was so wrong, He continued to do even more. God often uses people to do things on his behalf and the next day He sent a speaker to help others be delivered. She said that God had sent her to set a few women free. Free from what? Free from hurt. Free from anger. Free from depression. Free from anything in their lives that was holding them back from becoming who God called them to be. She walked around the room with a strong air of authority and announced, "The Holy Spirit said, 'Seven.'" What? Only seven? There were about 200 hundred women in the room and I am sure everyone had something they needed to be delivered from, whether they admitted it or not.

Everyone in the room was given a handout. It was a picture of a maze. In the maze were various pictures, strategically placed, and the objective was to find the way out of the maze. I started at the top and found my way through the pictures of the clouds, the mountains, the storm, the tornado, the forest, and finally, through the fire, before exiting the maze. I completed it quickly and sat quietly as others worked to find their way. As I sat waiting, I thought to myself how the maze symbolized life. You will face all types of situations, both good and bad, but you can and will find your way though, if you do not give up.

The speaker silently continued to walk around the room as everyone finished the maze. All of a sudden, she stopped directly in front of me. I was the first out of the seven women God had chosen to be delivered. It was my time for deliverance. She gently laid her hands on my chest and began to softly whisper in my ear. She said that she was going to speak to the spirit of confusion, the spirit of disappointment and the spirit of unworthiness. I was in awe. Do I have another spirit I wondered? She had chosen the word *unworthiness*. Had she read my journal? I know that was not the case. It was God. She rubbed me down with water from a make shift well at the front of the room. I felt as if water was pouring all over me, but it wasn't. It was barely a few drops. I did not understand what was happening. For what seems like several minutes, I had a vision of being on the beach with God. He held out His hands and I could feel and see my spirit leave my body and circle around Him. He said, "Shana, I am with you and won't leave you." Yes, He called MY name! The feeling was so calming and peaceful. I could feel Him wrap his arms around me like a mother would her newborn baby. The scent similar to lavender flowers filled the air. It was a pleasant and comforting aroma.

As I woke up from what I thought was a dream, I began to once again vomit the white foamy substance. It went on for a few minutes. What had just happened to me? What was happening now? Was God purging all the junk from my life? I was being delivered from spirits of hurt, confusion, and unworthiness. I had my first real experience with God and He had confirmed He would always be with me. You can be confident of this: Whether you are in the midst of a storm or just beginning to enter one, God is with you. My new relationship with God was beginning to take shape.

When beginning any relationship, the first phase is all about getting acquainted. I think this is one of the easiest phases in establishing a relationship with God. The instructions are simple: Read the Word. Find a Bible you are comfortable with and begin to read. It is just that simple. Read whenever you feel led, for as long as you feel led. At first, I often would find myself reading at five in the morning. There was something special about waking up and starting my day in the Word. The house was quiet, my mind was focused and I began to understand, with clarity, what once seemed so foreign to me. I was being filled with knowledge that helped me take on the daily challenges before me. If you are not sure where to begin reading, the Holy Spirit will guide and direct you. Set aside time every day to read the Word. Building a strong relationship requires getting to know the other person. God already knows all there is to know about you. Through reading

His Word, you will get to know Him better. The harder you work at it, the better it will be.

The next phase is expectation. Sit back and expect God to show up. He will begin to reveal things through His word. The more I read, the more I expected Him to reveal to me. Big results require big expectations; low or little expectations means little to no results. Your level of expectation is connected to your obedience. According to Deuteronomy 11:26-27, "Behold, I set before you today a blessing and a curse: the blessing, if you obey the commandments of the Lord your God which I command you today; and the curse, if you do not obey the commandments of the Lord your God, but turn aside from the way which I command you today, to go after other gods which you have not known." God will bless those who obey His command. It does not matter that you are not perfect. He knows exactly who you are and where you are. He loves your heart. He expects you to ask Him. Make your request and expect Him to work a miracle in your life. I know you may have doubts. I did too, at first. But the more He showed up, the more I began to trust Him, even though I could not see Him.

This is why I began to write down everything. I could see God in so many situations in my life and I did not want to forget anything. I also wanted to share the excitement of my journey with everyone, especially my children. I wanted to leave them nuggets of wisdom from my life lessons in hopes they would benefit from them and avoid some of the struggles I had faced. Apparently, God's plan was greater than my own because here I am sharing my journey with you.

As you read, mediate and allow the words to minister to you. During the process, you will be learning how to talk to your Father. I had a thirst that nothing else could fill. Something inside me kept pushing me to seek more. There was something in my life that was missing. I had all the things society said was ideal—nice car, beautiful home and good paying job—but I lacked satisfaction. Does this sound like anyone you know? You have everything, except the one thing you most desire? Salvation. Well, I am here to tell you, that everything you need is within us, if we are saved. Salvation is simply the deliverance of our sin by having faith in Jesus Christ. Without salvation, we are in desperate need of something we cannot tap into. We are lost and constantly searching for that missing thing in our lives.

The time has come to rise up and step into the new being you were created to be. As stated in 2 Corinthians 5:17, "Therefore if anyone is in Christ, he is a new creature; the old things passed away; behold, new things have come." God has chosen you and no man can stop you. You have been equipped to handle problems differently, in a godly manner. As a new creation, you will learn to lean on God Almighty. This special assignment was designed just for you. In this difficult season, you are birthing something that must be bought forth. God is going to use you just as you are. Do not be afraid to be criticized or judged. You are not alone. God is your protector. How can you know He is really there? Deuteronomy 31:6 reads, "Be strong and courageous. Do not be afraid or terrified because of them, for the LORD your God goes with you; he will never leave you nor forsake you." In every situation, He is in the midst. You will learn through your relationship with God to challenge everything in the spirit. Isaiah 54:17 advises us that, "No weapon formed against you shall prosper, and every tongue *which* rises against you in judgment you shall condemn. This *is* the heritage of the servants of the Lord, and their righteousness *is* from me,' says the Lord." Guess what? It's a fixed fight. God is guiding you. Rise up!

Scripture Reading:

John 4:10-14

Jesus answered and said unto her, If thou knewest the gift of God, and who it is that saith to thee, Give me to drink; thou wouldest have asked of him, and he would have given thee living water. The woman saith unto him, Sir, thou hast nothing to draw with, and the well is deep: from whence then hast thou that living water? Art thou greater than our father Jacob, which gave us the well, and drank thereof himself, and his children, and his cattle? Jesus answered and said unto her, Whosoever drinketh of this water shall thirst again: But whosoever drinketh of the water that I shall give him shall never thirst; but the water that I shall give him shall be in him a well of water springing up into everlasting life.

Affirmation:

No one has the same relationship with God. I will not compare myself to others. They do not have the same experiences and situations. Therefore, I cannot have the same relationship with God – its personal. There are some key characteristics needed for a good relationship such as trust, and communication. The same holds true with God. I need to trust Him and communicate with him through prayer, and studying his word.

Describe the best relationship you ever had. What made it great?

Thoughts:

_____

_____

_____

_____

_____

_____

_____

_____

_____

_____

_____

_____

_____

_____

What did you do to maintain that relationship?

Thoughts:

_____

_____

_____

_____

_____

_____

_____

_____

_____

_____

_____

_____

How does that relationship compare to the relationship you desire to have with God?

Thoughts:

_____

_____

_____

_____

What actions do you need to take to maintain a closer relationship with God? What or who do you need to remove from your life that is hindering your relationship with God?

_____

_____

_____

_____

_____

_____

_____

_____

_____

_____

_____

_____

_____

_____

_____

_____

_____

_____

_____

Prayer:

Father, I thank you for the knowledge and desire you have given me. I want a closer more personal relationship with you. A relationship that allows me to smile when I hurt, shout through my pain and still be able to praise you just because you are God Almighty. Continue to fill me with your grace and your mercy. Activate my gift. Please remove anyone and anything from my life that is seeking to destroy our relationship. Father, when I call on you please continue to comfort me in your arms and wipe my tears away. I cannot fight this battle without you. I need you. I want you. I love you. Amen.

Chapter 3 – What Have You Asked Him for Lately?

Take a look at your present situation, and ask yourself, "What do I need from God?" God is watching and listening. I wanted so desperately for God to save my child, to get him out of his current environment and to see him go to college. I had prayed for him not to be like several of the men in my family, drug dealers with no ambition or goals. I was determined. He would be successful. He would be the first male in several generations to graduate college. To the contrary, he was doing everything but the right thing. I would stay up at night worrying about things I had no control over. Why was God allowing my child to do these things? After all, my husband and I had done all the right things. We kept him in the best schools, gave him everything his heart desired, and we went to church. I was questioning God and wondering if He was even listening to my cries. Why was my son being spiritually attacked? Why was he allowing all these things to happen to him? To me? Had I done something wrong? Was I a bad parent? I was still struggling to understand and accept that if God was allowing things to be this way, it was because He knew what He was doing and He had a plan.

Listen, you are a child of the Most High God. If you need help, ASK HIM. The Bible tells us we are the head, not the tail. We are joint heirs with Jesus. You have a right to come boldly to the throne of grace, despite your need. Nothing is too hard for God. God will answer your prayers, but you may have to wait. No matter what your situation looks like, trust God. This was difficult for me to do, at first, but I began to see how God continued to show up in my life, despite my wavering faith.

As different situations came and went, the stronger my faith grew. The day before my son was set to leave for college, I went to noon-day prayer service at our church. There was a young lady asking for prayer for her and her son. Her situation sounded similar to mine and she was broken, too. I knew exactly what she was feeling. I had shed the same tears over my son. I was led to share my testimony of how God had turned my son's life around and he was headed to college the next day. God used me to encourage her to trust Him and to not give up on her son. I recalled telling her He was a promise keeper and He would do that no matter what was going on in our lives. Later that afternoon, I received a text from my son that read, "In jail." I was distraught. I drove home as quickly as I could and shared the news with my husband and best friend. I was so emotional, I threw myself on the ground and begged God to help me understand. I believed he was going to college. Earlier that year, I was talking with one of the ministers from my church about my concerns with my son. She warned me that he would get into trouble but now to worry because God has hands wrapped around him. This was very comforting to hear. She even said that he would not only graduate from college but would be a leader among the young. That was the plan for his life. Why else would God send a prophet to tell me he would go to school? Why else would God give him a full four-year academic scholarship?

I had spent an earlier portion of the day encouraging another mother who was asking the congregation for prayers for her son who was getting in trouble. I was so confident that God had answered my prayers, and now I was beginning to doubt God's promises. Later, I realized that he was being arrested at the exact same time that I was telling my story at church earlier that day. I spoke with such confidence and faith in what God had done for my son and encouraged so many others. And now he was in jail, the day before he was supposed to leave for college. I began praying, asking God to give me an understanding of what was happening. I was angry, embarrassed and hurt.

I began to yell and demand God to reveal Himself in the situation. In that moment, I heard the voice of God tell me to go into my son's bedroom. I got up from the grass in my backyard and went to his room. His instructions were clear. I was told to anoint a white bed sheet and to pray over all of my son's belongings which were piled in the middle of the floor, waiting to be packed the next day for college. As I anointed the sheet, I began to pray. I prayed for God to allow him to be released and able to go to school as planned. I prayed for Him to put the right judge on the stand, and allow him to see what a precious gift God had given me. I concluded my prayer and draped the sheet over all of his things.

The next morning, I removed the sheet and reminded God of His promises. Sometimes you have to remind God. No, he doesn't forget. He is omniscient, which means all knowing. When I say that I reminded him of His promises, I mean I used His Word to get his attention (Isaiah 43:26, Isaiah 55:11). I reminded God that He had promised my son would go to school and graduate. Two of my favorite scriptures that helped me through tough times were Jeremiah 29:11 and Romans 8:28. During this time, I recited them repeatedly. When we arrived at court, my son looked like a child disguised as a criminal. My hurt hung heavy, but I continued to recite my scriptures from Jeremiah and Romans. The attorney's plea was that my son had made a mistake. He was a good kid with a full academic scholarship of over $80,000 and he was scheduled to leave for college later that day. The judge looked at him and said, "You are too smart to keep getting in trouble! Lord, I hope I am making the right decision by giving you a PR bond." Yes, you read that correctly. God put the right judge before him; one who also called on the Lord. He delivered on His promise. He was released and we left for school.

Be encouraged. There will be tough times and everything may seem to be working against you, but do not give up. Remember that if God promised it, it will be done. Nothing you have done and nothing that has been said about you will change the way God sees you. Man may look at you and see an adulterer, sinner, liar, or cheater, BUT GOD sees His child, the same child he sent His Son Jesus to die on the cross for the remission of your sins. God will turn your situation around. He will allow certain situations to happen in your life. These situations not only are you learning but your faith is growing. Ask God to give you something to shout about. *BIG results require BIG expectations.* Surrender all your problems to Him and allow God to be God.

Scripture Reading:

Jeremiah 33: 1-3

While Jeremiah was still confined in the courtyard of the guard, the LORD gave him this second message: "This is what the LORD says—the LORD who made the earth, who formed and established it, whose name is the LORD: Ask me and I will tell you remarkable secrets you do not know about things to come.

Affirmation:

When I look at my current situation, I need God. Big results require big expectations. I will be faced with tough times but God is anxiously waiting for me to surrender them to Him. I can reflect on past situations and see how God was in the midst. I made it through. Every situation was not answered how I wanted but I know it is part of His plan. There is/was something to be gained.

What do you need from God today? What are you expecting God to do in your life? How will your life look, and feel differently?

Thoughts:

Prayer:

Lord, you know what I stand in need of. I am asking for your guidance. Please step in and give me clarity in this situation. Give me the right words to comfort me and the knowledge to do and say whatever is pleasing to you. Lord, I pray your will be done. I thank you in advance for endurance, grace and mercy. Amen.

Chapter 4 – I Surrender All

Why do we worry about how and when God will do what He's promised? Because worrying has become a habit and it is easier to do than trust. During this season of my life, it was hard dealing with everything that was going on. At times I was so overwhelmed all I could do was cry. I had begun to establish a relationship with God and sought Him for answers, but in some areas, I still struggled.

I was sick and tired of being sick and tired. I had a strong feeling that even though I did not feel good, I needed to go to our mid-week prayer service. It was raining and several of the streets near the church were flooded. Lots of so-called reasons for me to turn around but instead I pressed on. I arrived anticipating receiving a word that would comfort me. The minister was speaking on turning all our worries over to God. I sat and pondered over everything I was constantly worrying about. My mind was made up. I was giving all my problems to Him. I realized the problems with my family were the hardest for me to deal with. When things were not perfect with my son, I was brought to my lowest point. I blamed myself for how things were going. I questioned my parenting. Should I have said no? Did I do too much? Did I not do enough? Was it my fault that I did not make him go to church more often? So many questions; so few answers.

Life may be difficult. Correction: it will be difficult. But be encouraged and know you can give it all to God, because He cares and He is able. As I knelt at the altar, I prayed and asked God to make everything wrong in my life right. I asked him to take my problems and give me direction on how to help fix them. I stood up and returned to my seat, free from the weight of my problems.

Now is your time to surrender all to God. Activate your faith by believing that your situation is already done. Continue to want God to intervene on your behalf. Know that you know that you know God will answer your requests. Show your faith by speaking the word of God into your situation. Stop begging God and speak words of faith. Just as God said unto Moses at the Red Sea in Exodus 14:15-16, "Wherefore criest thou unto me? Speak unto the children of Israel that they go forward. But lift thou up thy rod, and stretch out thine hand over the sea, and divide it: and the children of Israel shall go on dry ground through the midst of the sea."

When God gives you a word, He gives you hope. He reminds us He has not forgotten His promise. When you surrendered your life to God, everything seemed to go crazy, right? Do not worry. That is perfectly normal. As a matter of fact, it is all part of the plan. The devil is angry. He is desperately trying to stop you from fulfilling your purpose. Continue praising God. The road will not be easy, but you cannot give up on your journey because something inside will not let you. That something is the Holy Spirit. He will continue to grow in you and to open your spiritual eyes but you must continue to surrender your all to Him. God is building your faith—walk like it is done, talk like it is done, act like it is done, and pray like it is done. The greatest example of faith is being able to praise God in the midst of your worst situation. Did you know YOUR praise has the power to destroy the enemy? That is the key to your deliverance. Surrender it all to God, your problems and your praise.

Today I challenge you to write a letter to God. Begin by giving him thanks for all things he has done, is doing, and is going to do in your life. Ask Him to help you with your breakthrough. Be specific. Be clear. Proverbs 18:21 tells us there is power in our tongues. As you write your letter, speak the words aloud and you shall see the fruit thereof. There is power in your tongue. We serve a mighty God who can and will do mighty things on our behalf. Be bold. Instead of asking to be able to pay the rent, ask God for a new house with no mortgage. Do not just ask for Him to help your child behave better, ask for salvation and deliverance. Let go and let God. Make your requests known to the Lord. Luke 11:9-10 says, "And I say unto you, Ask, and it shall be given you; seek, and ye shall find; knock, and it shall be opened unto you. For every one that asked receiveth; and he that seeketh findeth; and to him that knocketh it shall be opened." Expect it, believe it, and celebrate it.

Scripture Reading:

1 Chronicles 4:9-10

There was a man named Jabez who was more honorable than any of his brothers. His mother named him Jabez because his birth had been so painful. He was the one who prayed to the God of Israel, "Oh that you would bless me and expand my territory! Please be with me in all that I do, and keep me from all trouble and pain!" And God granted him his request.

Affirmation:

Worrying is a bad habit and sometimes it is easier to worry than to trust God. Today, I will replace worry with faith. I will remind God of his promise to never leave me or forsake me. I will replace negative thoughts and words with positive affirmations and praise.

What areas of your life do you need to trust God more?

___
___
___
___
___
___
___
___
___
___
___
___

_____
_____
_____
_____
_____
_____
_____

Write your letter to God. Be specific. Be clear. Remember words have power. Be careful what you pray for. Expect it, believe it, and celebrate it.

Thoughts:

Dear God,

_____
_____
_____
_____
_____

Prayer:

Lord, I surrender all to you. Today I give you my all. I give you me, my problems, my concerns, my health, my marriage, my children, my finances, my fears, my future and my everything. Your word said says ask and it shall be given to me. I am asking that you keep your arms wrapped around my family and me. I thank you Lord in advance. Amen

Chapter 5 – Let Us Pray

We ask ourselves, "What is prayer?" Prayer is communication between you and God. I grew up in a church where the older women were considered to have what everyone considered to be *powerful* prayers. Their prayers contained every cliché they could recall from as far back as their childhoods plus countless scripture references. I often found myself lost and confused trying to follow along as they prayed. Well I am here to tell you, your prayer is personal. There is nothing wrong with corporate prayer, but it should not take the place of your personal prayer time. It is during this time, you build and strengthen your own relationship with God. Talking to God is as easy as talking to your best friend. What makes it even better is that He is a better listener than you could ever imagine.

Every Friday for about six weeks, something negative had occurred related to my son. It was time for that to change. I created a Facebook event and invited several people to join me in prayer the next Friday evening at 9PM. I wanted to bombard heaven with prayer requests for my son and all other children who needed prayer. After that first call to prayer, I began praying every Friday night at 9PM. Whether I was in a meeting, having dinner with family or in the middle of a party, when my alarm alerted me at 8:55PM, I stopped everything and went to myself to pray. I consistently prayed for God to cover and guide my children. I begged God to remove anything and anyone that was not like Him in their lives. I asked God to put a hedge of protection around them and not allow any hurt, harm or danger to come upon them and that they would not bring any upon anyone else.

I encountered so many broken mothers going through the same situation with their children as I was with mine. I began praying for their strength and their children. I asked many of them to join me in my prayer battle to save our children. The list of prayer warriors grew so long I had to keep a list. Wanting to keep track of everyone, I added pictures. My Friday night prayer time was set aside for me to ask God to cover these troubled children. I was determined to speak life into them. I refused to curse them by labeling them as lost and confused. I chose to speak blessings over them.

God desires us to pray. You may have been praying over and over about the same issue and feel God is not listening, but He is. He is always listening. Something worth considering is how effective is your prayer? It is important to speak God's language, His Word. This is why reading and studying the Bible is so important. How else will you know what to ask for and how? The Bible tells you so. Joshua 1:8 says, "This Book of the Law shall not depart from your mouth, but you shall meditate on it day and night, so that you may be careful to do according to all that is written in it. For then you will make your way prosperous, and then you will have good success." Prayer gives you a different perspective on your situation. Step back and take a look at what is currently going on around you. What do you see? Use your spiritual not natural eyes. Do not react to what you see, just pray and wait. Remind yourself that God can do anything and that you are not alone. In the book of 1 Chronicles, we are reminded we should not be afraid or discouraged for the Lord God is with us and will not fail or forsake us. "And David said to his son Solomon, "Be strong and of good courage, and do *it;* do not fear nor be dismayed, for the Lord God—my God—*will be* with you. He will not leave you nor forsake you, until you have finished all the work for the service of the house of the Lord."

Do you find yourself waking up at night, feeling restless? God has not awakened you for a snack or trip to the bathroom. God is seeking your undivided attention. There is power to be found in the midnight hour. Midnight is the darkest hour of the day. It is the point when the transition darkness into light begins. This is symbolically a special time to fight whatever you are dealing with. Speak light into your midnight. The world is still and God is waiting eagerly to hear from you. How do I know this? Because there are numerous biblical references to midnight prayers.

In Acts 16, Paul and Silas are beaten and thrown into jail for casting out an evil spirit from a girl who had been taunting them. They are jailed for doing what God required of them. Instead of complaining to God, they praise Him. I am sure the other prisoners probably thought they were crazy. In a seemingly hopeless situation, God steps in. At midnight, an earthquake shakes the prison causing the doors to swing open and freeing them from their chains.

You may be feeling chained to your current situation. People around you are doubting whether or not you will make it through. Those chains can and will be broken through faith and praise. Right where you are, right now, in the midst of it all, start praising God. Your praise will draw you closer to God, closer to the resolution of your situation. No matter what the situation is, it will line up with God's plan and the chains are broken. Whether your prison is being bound to financial debt, bound to physical pain or family problems, He is able to set you free. Praise Him.

Scripture Reading:

Matthew 6:9-13

"This, then, is how you should pray: 'Our Father in heaven, hallowed be your name, your kingdom come, your will be done, on earth as it is in heaven. Give us today our daily bread. And forgive us our debts, as we also have forgiven our debtors. And lead us not into temptation, but deliver us from the evil one.'"

1 Timothy 2:1-2

I urge, then, first of all, that petitions, prayers, intercession and thanksgiving be made for all people—for kings and all those in authority, that we may live peaceful and quiet lives in all godliness and holiness.

Affirmation:

Prayer is communication between God and I. It sometimes gives me a different perspective on my situation. God desires me to pray and study. I know when I am struggling I can count on others to pray with and for me.

Write out a prayer regarding a situation that you need guidance, clarity or are concerned about.

_____
_____
_____
_____
_____
_____
_____
_____
_____
_____
_____

What will you do to remember to pray more at the start of the day, throughout the day or at night?

Thoughts:

When you need another spirit filled person to pray with or for you, who will you call?

Prayer:

Lord, I thank you, thank you, thank you. Words cannot express how grateful I am to have you. You are marvelous. You are awesome. You are my everything. Thank you for allowing me to awaken at this midnight hour. In the midst of my mess, I thank you. I thank you for our renewed and refreshed relationship. Thank you for breaking the chains. Amen.

Chapter 6 – Fasting

There are some things in life that will not and cannot be broken without fasting. Fasting is refraining from food or drink for a specified period of time for a spiritual purpose. Fasting invokes God to act. It also brings you closer to God. He honors your sacrifice and as a result creates a more intimate relationship. During fasting, you have more one on one time with God. As you fast, your thoughts become clearer, His voice louder and the Word more meaningful.

So when should you fast? There are several reasons why a person should fast. First reason is just to praise and worship God. In Luke 2:37, the widow expressed her love to God by fasting and praying night and day. You can also deepen your relationship with God. Romans 12:1-2 states, "Therefore, I urge you, brothers and sisters, in view of God's mercy, to offer your bodies as a living sacrifice, holy and pleasing to God—this is your true and proper worship. Do not conform to the pattern of this world, but be transformed by the renewing of your mind. Then you will be able to test and approve what God's will is—his good, pleasing and perfect will." If you are seeking guidance and direction from God, fast and pray. James 1:5, "If any of you lacks wisdom, let him ask of God, who gives to all liberally and without reproach, and it will be given to him."

When you combine prayer and fasting you create a powerful recipe for change. They make the enemy mad. Fasting is an expected component of a Christian walk. It is crucial to continued spiritual growth. We can fast for God's intervention as David did on behalf of his sick child in 2 Samuel 12:15-17: "Then Nathan departed to his house. And the Lord struck the child that Uriah's wife bore to David, and it became ill. David therefore pleaded with God for the child, and David fasted and went in and lay all night on the ground. So the elders of his house arose *and went* to him, to raise him up from the ground. But he would not, nor did he eat food with them."

There are four types of fasts. God honors all kinds of fasts. To determine the best fast for you, go to the Master himself, in prayer, and await his instruction. I would also suggest that you partner with your physician before beginning any fast, especially if you have any chronic illnesses or are taking any medication.

4 Types of Fasts	
Normal or Regular	During this fast, you refrain from food and only consume water.
Absolute	No food or water but not to exceed three days.
Partial	Limited eating, mostly vegetables and grains with no meat.
Rational	Eating or omitting certain foods during certain times of the day.

When you have received your instructions from the Holy Spirit, you can begin to prepare yourself physically for the fast. Plan changes to you daily schedule that will allow you to focus on God without too many distractions. Preparing meals in advance and setting aside a designated time and space for quiet time with God (to pray and hear from Him) are two great areas to make changes in before starting a fast. If you will be fasting alone, take time to explain your family what you will be doing, what it means to you, and also how it may impact them. Even with proper preparation, you still may find yourself faced with a potential challenge: resisting the temptation to eat food that you have prepared for the family. Afraid you will not be able to resist? I can tell you from experience, "Yes, you can!" You know your purpose and you have a predesigned plan. All you have to do is stick to it! If you feel you need support or encouragement along the way, ask your *spiritual* friends to hold you accountable and keep you uplifted in prayer. One word of warning, pray about who you tell that you are fasting. Not everyone needs to know you are fasting. The enemy is listening and he will try to deter you in any way he can (Ephesians 6:12). Your focus should be on God during this time, not the fact that you are fasting and not able to eat. This is a time of personal reflection and spiritual growth between you and your Father.

The next step in the fasting process is making spiritual preparations. While you will be denying yourself food, your intake of spiritual nutrition is about to soar. Dedicated time for prayer and reading God's Word will be the keys to a successful fast. The sacrifice may seem great, but the reward will be far greater.

Jesus made the same promise to us regarding fasting that He made concerning prayer. In Matthew 6:16-18, we read, "Moreover, when you fast, do not be like the hypocrites, with a sad countenance. For they disfigure their faces that they may appear to men to be fasting. Assuredly, I say to you, they have their reward. But you, when you fast, anoint your head and wash your face, so that you do not appear to men to be fasting, but to your Father who is in the secret place; and your Father who sees in secret will reward you openly." Whether you are fasting simply to praise God, for deepened relationships or instructions, our heavenly Father will reward you. There are several blessings in fasting. The first benefit is a closer personal relationship with God. You will notice while fasting that all of your senses are heightened. You will hear, see and feel God's presence like never before. I recommend keeping a journal of your experience. This will allow you a chance to reflect on your journey and to relive the God-inspired experiences you had along the way.

Another benefit of fasting is it reinforces for us just how much we need God in our lives, and not just in the physical sense. It humbles us and changes our lives for the better.

Isaiah 58:11 reveals, "The Lord will guide you always; he will satisfy your needs in a sun-scorched land and will strengthen your frame. You will be like a well-watered garden, like a spring whose waters never fail." Fasting ushers in season of deliverance and breakthrough based on God's promises.

This is probably one of the most life-changing and God-affirming aspects of a fast.

I completed my first fast earlier this year. God laid on my heart to do a 21-day fast. Rebel that I am, I asked him several times to confirm that this was what He truly wanted from me. By the time I began, I was confident I had heard Him clearly and correctly. I shared with a few spiritual friends about the fast and asked that they join me, if God directed them to. Whether they joined me or not, I wanted them to pray that I would be able to sustain the fast.

Before beginning my fast, I set out to identify what exactly I needed God's help with. For a variety of reasons, I knew the focus of my prayers would be my family, but on a deeper level, standing in the gap for my oldest son really tugged at my heart. I was in constant prayer for God to keep His hands upon him and to deliver him completely from the life he was living. I began in faith and continued my sacrifice for 21 days.

Shortly after completing my fast, a heavy feeling rested on my heart. My husband asked me several times what was wrong. I struggled to put it into words. It was like nothing I had ever experienced before. I felt compelled to pray, but with a sense of urgency I still cannot explain. In obedience, I did as God commanded. I did all I knew to do. I prayed. Every day, all day, I prayed. On September 23, I understood the why behind the season of prayer.

Shortly before midnight, that inexplicable feeling returned and thoughts of my son intensified. I had not spoken to him in a few days so I decided to text him to ask if he was okay. Why is it teenagers never feel the need to reply as soon as they get a text from their parents? After some time passed, I prayed, "God, I don't understand what is going on, but I trust you. I ask that you continue to keep your hands on him. Do not allow him to be hurt or anyone by his hands and I understand that you are using him but please no more jail. Amen." After, I finished praying I felt a sense of relief and comfort. Then, I went to sleep. Around 1AM, my husband's phone rang. I could see the caller ID; it was our oldest son. My husband put the call on speaker and as my son explained the altercation, I panicked and cried. Yes, I temporarily gave into my flesh. He went on to say that he was not seriously hurt and neither was the other party. He added he was not under arrest for anything." After the call ended, I laid in silence reflecting on the strong feeling I had earlier and my prayer. I knew that through fasting and prayer, I had petitioned to God to protect him. And God delivered and answered my prayers. I then began to praise Him. I began to pray out loud, which I rarely did. I could feel the presence of the Holy Spirit.

As I laid back down and closed my eyes, I heard a voice say, "Jehovah-Jireh. Rest. I've got him. Jehovah-Jireh. He will see me. Rest. I am the only Almighty One. I have my hands on him." I knew there were over 100 names of God, but was unfamiliar with *Jehovah-Jireh*. I grabbed my cell phone to do a quick search and the results said, "Provider," and referenced the story of Abraham and Isaac found in Genesis 22. Abraham's willingness to offer his son Isaac as a sacrifice to God demonstrated his faith. In verse 13, God honored Abraham's obedience and willingness by providing a ram to be offered as the burnt offering instead of Isaac.

What are you willing to sacrifice for a closer relationship with God? Are you willing to entrust Him with your most prized possessions? Your children? Your marriage? Your faith? Take a moment to think about some of the things you have been asking God for that He seems not to be providing. As the Scripture Reading that follows tells us, some things REQUIRE fasting and prayer before being manifested in our lives. If what you want is worth having, now is the time for fasting and prayer. Focus on God's promises. Be obedient and faithful to His instruction and know that He will be faithful to you It's time to fast and pray. Focus on the promises of GOD. He will confirm his promise.

Scripture Reading:

Matthew 17: 20-21

So Jesus said to them, "Because of your unbelief; for assuredly, I say to you, if you have faith as a mustard seed, you will say to this mountain, 'Move from here to there,' and it will move; and nothing will be impossible for you. However, this kind does not go out except by prayer and fasting."

Affirmation:

There are some things in life that will not and cannot be broken without fasting. I will pray and ask God for guidance on if, when, and what type of fast to begin. I will dedicate time for prayer and reading God's Word.

How often will you pray? When will you study?

Thoughts:

What topics would you like to learn more about and why?

Thoughts:

Prayer:

Lord, as I begin this journey of fasting, please give me clear instructions on the fast that will bring forth a closer relationship with you and the breakthrough that my heart desires. Give me strength to endure any and all temptation that I will encounter. No sacrifice on my part can compare to the sacrifice you made for me by dying on the cross, but I will honor you with my fast and willingly sacrifice to you. Amen.

Chapter 7 – Promises of God

As I read and studied God's Word, I began to understand His promises better. The Holy Spirit directed me to read the story of Abraham. Abraham was ninety-nine years old when God came to him and made him three promises. Genesis 12:1-3, "Now the Lord had said to Abram: 'Get out of your country, from your family and from your father's house, to a land that I will show you. I will make you a great nation; I will bless you and make your name great; and you shall be a blessing. I will bless those who bless you, and I will curse him who curses you; and in you all the families of the earth shall be blessed." A promise from God is an agreement, also known as a covenant. One of God's covenants to Abraham was that He would keep His promise to him regarding his descendants becoming a great nation. However, God may ask and require you to do things in order for the promise to be fulfilled. God commanded Abraham to take his only son Isaac and offer him for a burnt offering. As a parent, I can only imagine at the moment how hurt and pained Abraham felt, yet he still did as he was instructed to do. Because of his obedience, God provided a ram in the bush to be sacrificed instead of his son.

There is no expiration on God's promises. The enemy will use any tactics he can to convince you otherwise, but if God has promised you something, nothing can change that. Psalm 89:34 promises, "My covenant I will not break, nor alter the word that has gone out of my lips." Not only will his promise never fail. Instead of allowing the enemy to distract you, stay focused on the promises of God and trust Him to get you through any situation. Continue to pray. The promise is yours. Wait for it!

Scripture Reading:

Deuteronomy 28:9

The LORD will establish you as his holy people, as he promised you on oath, if you keep the commands of the LORD your God and walk in obedience to him.

Genesis 17:4-8

"As for me, this is my covenant with you: You will be the father of many nations. No longer will you be called Abram; your name will be Abraham, for I have made you a father of many nations. I will make you very fruitful; I will make nations of you, and kings will come from you. I will establish my covenant as an everlasting covenant between me and you and your descendants after you for the generations to come, to be your God and the God of your descendants after you. The whole land of Canaan, where you now reside as a foreigner, I will give as an everlasting possession to you and your descendants after you; and I will be their God."

Affirmation:

A promise from God is an agreement, also known as a covenant. There is not expiration on God's promises. I will expect God's promise to be fulfilled.

There are several promises from God in the bible. Find and write down at least 3.

Thoughts:

_____

_____

_____

_____

_____

When have you seen these promises in your life?

_____

_____

_____

_____

_____

Prayer:

Lord, I thank you for the promise. I shall not be moved. I am standing on your Word. In spite of the opposition, I will walk by faith and not by sight. I believe that you will prevail. I will receive all my promises. I declare and decree many blessings upon myself, my children, my children's children, and everyone around me. In Jesus' name, Amen.

Chapter 8 – The Wait

Like it or not, life is going to send trials your way. In order to survive them, you will have to learn to be patient and to wait on God. He has promised to always be there. Better yet, He's omnipotent. He is ALREADY there. You may have not sensed His presence at first, but know that He is there.

Waiting is not easy, and truth be told, I have been known to be a little impatient at times. Not to long after giving birth to my youngest son, I ran into a young lady I had previously worked with. She asked if I had applied at this telecommunications company. She shared that during her recent interview, she saw my name on a piece of paper on the interviewer's desk. I told her there must be someone else with the same name, because I had not applied or interviewed with them. The job I had was not very fulfilling, but I earned enough to take care of my financial obligations.

A few weeks later, I opened the Sunday paper, and the first thing I saw was an advertisement for the same telecommunications company. They were hiring for a customer service representative position. I had never heard of the company until my former coworker mentioned it in conversation weeks before. Was it a sign? It was around 8PM Sunday evening when I decided to go online and apply. Around 8AM the next morning, my phone rang. It was the recruiter. He had received my application and wanted me to come in for an interview, TODAY. Over the course of the next few hours, I interviewed, took a typing test—followed by a drug test—and was hired on the spot.

Not only did I exceed expectations, I received my first promotion within less than a year. I was focused on my career and wanted to continue moving up within the company. Over the next few years, I earned several promotions. Not only was I enjoying my work, but also a successful career.

One day my team leader approached me with an opportunity to take on an interim position for a couple of months. I was excited. Beyond excited, actually. Of course I would do it. I had started at the bottom and now I would be second in command of a call center staffed by over 600 people. The position would only last a couple of months but the potential leadership experience it would bring made it worth it. I was even more excited a few months later when the position came open for applicants. I had maintained my faith in what God had promised me and this was an opportunity that I could not allow to pass me. Proverbs 3:5 states, "Trust in the LORD with all thine heart; and lean not unto thine own understanding." As excited as I was, I wanted to remain committed and obedient to what God wanted me to do.

Often, we pray and then act on our own accord, not waiting for God's answer. That behavior can get us in trouble. I petitioned God for confirmation that it was His Will for me to apply. I was unsure. After all, I had only done the job for two months. I waited and waited to hear from Him. Confirmation came one night while I was in bed. I heard Him say that I would be promoted, but in an unusual way. I had my answer! I jumped out of bed and applied for the position.

When the invitation to interview came two days later, I was so excited I went out and purchased a new suit. I was confident about my chances and wanted to interview in person, which meant driving almost three hours. It was worth the sacrifice to me. The entire way there, I prayed for God's will to be done. I arrived about a half hour early. As I sat in my car in the parking lot, I asked God not to allow me to embarrass myself and to help me answer every question with the knowledge and expertise required of the position. I anointed myself from head to toe and made sure my hands were covered with oil so my handshake would be extra special. In my heart I recited every scripture I could recall, took a deep breath and went inside.

I nailed the interview. It was the best one I had ever had. Afterwards, I was taken on a tour of the facilities and introduced to the management team I would be working with. As everything wrapped up, I knew this job was mine. I was so sure I had the job that when I got home, I began packing our belongings for relocation. After all, I had prayed, heard the voice of God, and He said I would be promoted.

Imagine my excitement two weeks later when the phone rang and the caller ID showed the info for the Site Director I had interviewed with. I quickly answered the phone, almost unable to contain my excitement. He told me I had done a phenomenal job interviewing, and I thought to myself, "Come on with the offer!" He went on to say I definitely had what it would take to be effective in the position, but he found someone else he felt was a better fit. What?! My mind was spinning. This could not be happening. This was my job. God had told me so. My house was packed and we were ready to move. I thanked him for the opportunity and hung up the phone. I was confused by what had just happened. I knew what God promised me, and if this position was not meant to be mine, so be it. My promotion was still on its way. I returned to my previous position and worked harder than ever. After a few weeks of navigating around our packed and ready to relocate home, my husband asked if the time had come to unpack. Without missing a beat, I told him we would not be unpacking because we were going to be moving. My response surprised him, but he stood in agreement with me.

Six months passed before I received a call that the position was open again for applicants. It was highly unusual for the same position to open up again so quickly at the same location. Typically, when someone is promoted, they hold the position for at least two to three years, if not longer. Without giving it another thought, I reapplied. This time, the promotion was mine. God said I would be promoted, but in an unusual way. Once again, He had been faithful to His promise.

When God makes you a promise, do not allow anticipation to make you anxious. Be patient, trust His timing and wait. Stepping outside of God's will of God can lead to you suffering unnecessary consequences. If I had exhibited a bad attitude or allowed my performance to suffer, I would not have been considered for the job. Because I trusted God and waited for Him to fulfill His promise to me, He did. Wait on God. His timing is perfect.

Scripture Reading:

Psalm 37:7-9

Rest in the LORD, and wait patiently for him: fret not thyself because of him who prospereth in his way, because of the man who bringeth wicked devices to pass. Cease from anger, and forsake wrath: fret not thyself in any wise to do evil. For evildoers shall be cut off: but those that wait upon the LORD, they shall inherit the earth.

Affirmation:

Like it or not, life is going to send trials my way. I will survive them. I will be patient and wait on God. He has promised to be there.

What are you waiting for God to do? What will you do while you wait?

Thoughts:

Prayer:

Lord, the wait is not easy. I cannot and will not do it without you. Lord, my heart desires for you to fill me up with more of you. In every situation, I will wait for your guidance and direction. Give me the endurance and strength to wait on you. In Jesus' name, Amen.

Chapter 9 – The Attack

As you go through the wait, you will be tested. Even writing this, I have to laugh. But of course at the time it was hardly a laughing matter. At the time of my attack everything that could go wrong, seemed to all go wrong at the same time. My husband and I were not necessarily the happiest couple, our oldest son seemed to be lost in the wilderness, and my job had become stressful. I was frustrated and overwhelmed with life. What could I do? Yep, you guessed it—prayed and waited, waited and prayed, and when I got tired, prayed and waited some more.

One Monday evening, while getting my hair braided, I received a private Facebook message from the well renowned Bishop T.D. Jakes. To those of you who may not know Bishop T.D. Jakes, he is an author, filmmaker and pastor of a non-denominational megachurch. I was completely shocked that he would actually be contacting me. Bishop T.D. Jakes actually had sent me a message. I had prayed a couple of weeks ago and the Holy Spirit told me to pray daily at 6AM. Was this my confirmation? Was God answering my prayers? It was so deep I have to share with you the exact transcript:

Conversation started October 29, 2012
Bishop Jakes   10/29, 6:23pm
hello beloved

Me   10/29, 6:23pm
hello. Wow. I can't believe you are online with me.

Bishop Jakes   10/29, 6:24pm
how are you doing today

Me   10/29, 6:24pm
I am having a rough day actually.

Bishop Jakes   10/29, 6:25pm
The Lord is your strength

Bishop Jakes   10/29, 6:25pm
Beloved in Christ, The Bible says, "Blessed is the man who listens to me, watching daily at my doors, waiting at my doorway" (Proverbs 8:34). The Lord shall bless us according to this Bible verse. The time has come for us walk on the heavenly realms. The Lord shall fill us with every spiritual blessing (Ephesians 1:3). He shall help us to ride on the heights of the land (Deuteronomy 32:13). I am standing in gap with you. I want you to pray this prayer by 6:00 AM for two days and get back to me ASAP; Prayer: Loving Lord Jesus, I come to your holy presence with humility. I surrender my life to You. I rely only on You. Have compassion on me and bless me. Come and abide in me. Sanctify me with your blood. Fill me with your power. Help me to forsake the worldly ways. Give me the grace to

inherit your divine nature. Transform me into your likeness. Fill me with every spiritual blessing. Perform miracles in my life and honor me before all eyes. In Your matchless name I pray. Amen.

Me   10/29, 6:28pm
Yes, sir! I will definitely do so. I know GOD sent you to me tonight. I am so filled right now. I don't know what to say, but thank you.

Bishop Jakes   10/29, 6:28pm
God bless you beloved. you shall testify. Are you ready for God's blessings this new month of November? There is a next step of faith I want you to take seriously after saying the prayers above to God and you will see the greatest gift of the lord upon your life this new month of November.

Me   10/29, 6:29pm
Thank you sir. I pray continue to cover and protect you. Thank you for being a vessel. I will contact you in two days.

Bishop Jakes   10/29, 6:29pm
The Lord is with you

Me   10/29, 6:29pm
Yes, I am very ready!

Bishop Jakes   10/29, 6:30pm
God bless you

Me   10/29, 6:30pm

Same to you!

Bishop Jakes   10/29, 6:31pm
I WANT TO PRAY FOR YOU AND I WANT YOU TO OPEN UP YOUR HEART WHILE WE SAY THESE PRAYERS, "And my God shall supply all your need according to His riches in glory by Christ Jesus". Philippians 4:19
Say this prayer with me. "The Just shall live by Faith" Habakkuk 2:4. Heavenly Father! I praise you and honor You! I thank You for being with me always and loving me with Your eternal love! You are in control of all things and I thank You for that. O Lord! Your Scripture clearly tells that without faith I can neither please You nor receive any answer for my prayer. Please forgive me for not believing in Your love, power and goodness. Many times I've been discouraged by my circumstances and many times I have failed to trust in You. Please forgive me Lord! You are the God of all hope and I acknowledge that nothing is too difficult for You. I am confident that You will meet all my needs as I seek to live according to Your word! Thank You Lord for helping me get over my unbelief removing all my fears and anxieties! Let me not lose heart on seeing the circumstances Lord! Strengthen my faith through which alone I can receive miracles from You Lord. You have said whatever I ask in prayer, believing, I will receive. Thank You for this promise Lord! I love You and trust in Your awesome power! I know You are with me right now to take care of my needs and I thank You for that. In Jesus' name I pray. Amen.

Me   10/29, 6:33pm
Amen

Bishop Jakes   10/29, 6:37pm
God bless you beloved. Beloved of God, when I was praying with you, the Holy Spirit revealed a revelation about you to me he said to tell you to pray harder every day and you should expect his supernatural blessings all the way.

Me   10/29, 6:43pm
Thank you Bishop. Thank you. Thank you.

Bishop Jakes   10/29, 6:46pm
The Lord is your strength beloved

Me   10/29, 6:48pm
Yes he is!! I have clear instructions now and I will continue to follow them.

Bishop Jakes   10/29, 6:51pm
You shall testify to the Glory of God upon your life

As you can see, I was so excited to hear a word. I wanted to hear from God so bad that the enemy showed up in the midst of my wait. Read a little further and I'll explain how the devil tried to trick me.

October 31, 2012
Me   10/31, 7:26am
Gm. I just wanted to say thank you. I have prayed the prayers above at 6am for the last two days. Last night

my husband opened up and admitted what was wrong with him. In the midst of it all. I prayed for him to be released and delivered from strong holds and anything not like God.

Bishop Jakes   10/31, 9:26am
AMEN
I SAW IT COMING BELOVED BUT I NEVER WANTED YOU TO KNOW LIKE THIS THE LORD IS YOUR STRENGTH BELOVED YOU SHALL BE SAVED

Me   10/31, 9:27am
But I need to know will my marriage be saved.

Bishop Jakes   10/31, 9:46am
YES BELOVED IT WILL
BY THE GRACE OF JESUS
THERE ARE THINGS YOU NEED TO DO NOW FOR THE GLORY OF GOD TO COME THROUGH IN YOUR LIFE

Me   10/31, 10:04am
Thx u
I will pray for God to show me what to do.

Bishop Jakes   10/31, 10:15am
BELOVED I WANT YOU TO GET AN ANOINTED OIL AND A SEED OF $200 THAT YOU WILL HAVE TO SOW TO AN ORPHANAGE HOME

Me   10/31, 10:15am
Ok. I will go now

Bishop Jakes   10/31, 10:16am
GOD BLESS YOU
YOU WILL SEND THE SUM OF $200 TO AN ORPHANAGE HOME WHO HAVE BEEN THROUGH SO MUCH HARDSHIP BELOVED AND YOU SHALL TESTIFY

Me   10/31, 10:17am
I will. I know where I need to go.

Bishop Jakes   10/31, 10:18am
I WILL FORWARD THE DETAILS TO YOU NOW WHICH YOU HAVE TO SOW YOUR DONATIONS TO

Me   10/31, 10:18am
Ok

As you can see I was even more hurt and shocked. I had prayed and prayed and asked God to send a word to me. I did get a word but it was not from God. I was confused and overwhelmed with pain. I didn't know what to do. I grabbed my keys and purse and got in my car. I drove around for a while, it seemed like hours. I was excited, scared and didn't quite know what to do. Was God telling me to do this? He knows my financial situation. All kinds of thoughts were running through my head. Would I miss out on my blessings because I was afraid to take a chance? My phone rang and I was crying hysterically. It was my aunt and she could immediately tell I was not my normal, chipper self. I couldn't explain everything I was feeling at that moment. I told her I couldn't talk and would call her later.

When I finally stopped driving, I was in front of my church and as I was sitting there something inside me keep pushing me to go inside. Well, I did. I went into the sanctuary it was quiet and so calming. I went straight to the altar and fell on my knees. I had my keys in one hand and my phone in the other. As I knelt at the altar, I began to pray for God to give me confirmation. I asked for clear instructions where I would not have any doubt on what he wanted me to do. I concluded with Amen. And then I heard my phone messenger beep. As I continued to knelt, I looked and saw the below message:

Bishop Jakes   10/31, 10:18am
You can make a wire transfer to them via Western Union Money Transfer (WUMT) OR MoneyGram Money Order (MGMO) with this details below;
Names: Umukoro Eguonor Country: Nigeria State; Delta State City;Warri Text Question: God bless? Text Answer: Your Family.
Send me the following details after you have made the wire transfer so I can forward it to them

Amount: Sender's name: Money Transfer Control Number (MTCN): Text Question: Text Answer: sender's Location; Sender's Phone number;

Bishop Jakes 10/31, 10:18am
I WANT YOU TO GO NOW AND SEND YOUR DONATIONS TO THEM AND GET BACK TO ME FOR MORE INSTRUCTIONS BELOVED
YOUR PROBLEMS WILL BE CHANGED TO HAPPINESS IN THE NAME OF JESUS

Me 10/31, 12:03pm
The devil is a liar!! U had me fooled. This is not the Bishop.

I could not believe this! I was so upset. I began to cry even harder. I had shared this story with so many people on how God had answered my prayers and how he used T.D. Jakes, such a great man of God to send a word to me. I was temporarily blinded! Then I stopped. At the very moment I concluded my prayer because God did exactly what I had asked for. He gave me confirmation that this was not from Him. Thank you God for showing up right on time!

As I got up to leave the sanctuary, the Pastor of our church approached the altar and helped me to my feet. He sat me down on the pew and asked me what was wrong. I shared EVERYTHING that was going on and he began to tell me his story. It was exactly my story. He gave me words of comfort and advised me to trust and wait on the Lord. At that very moment, a sense of peace and calmness came over me. I wiped my eyes and left the church. I made up my mind that the devil would not have the last laugh. He would not have any victory over me. I was not ashamed of what happened and called and told everyone how he tried to trick me. I was confident that God would continue to be with me. Psalm 23 reads Yea, though I walk through the valley of the shadow of death, I will fear no evil: for thou art with me, thy rod and thy staff the comfort me." That same night I received this message:

> *Bishop Jakes*   10/31, 6:33pm
> WHY DO HAVE DOUBT ALL OVER YOUR HEART BELOVED
>
> *Me*   10/31, 6:55pm
> Heavenly Father, I bind up anything that is not of you and send it back to the pits of hell. I curse every demonic spirit that approaches me. I will seek God my savior for victory. And that's paid for when Jesus died on the cross. Devil go to hell
>
> *Bishop Jakes*   10/31, 7:18pm
> THE LORD IS WITH YOU BELOVED
>
> *End of Conversation*

Boy did that sure feel good. I felt victorious! That night my husband and I had a talk and I felt the holy spirit awaken inside and take over me. Without hesitation, I laid my hands on his chest and began to pray. I prayed like I had never prayed before. From what I can recall, I prayed against the spirit of depression, hurt, conflict, and confusion. I had a strong physical feeling of something stirring up inside of me. My prayer changed. It is hard to describe but it definitely was not me and my ordinary Sunday school Bible prayers. When I finished praying, I went into the bathroom and began to throw up. The enemy had tried to push us apart by causing problems in our marriage but what he actually did was push us closer together. I was given the opportunity to pray for God to release anything that was hindering our relationship that had been ordained by Him. At this moment, we made a promise not to allow anything or anyone to come between our relationship. No longer would we allow the attack of the enemy to be a problem in our marriage.

Problems or attack of the enemy will always exist. As you are going through your situation, step back and determine the purpose of your problem. There are five purposes of problems: salvation, holiness, worship, praise and suffering.

Problems often push us closer to God. I am sure it's just me but when I was faced with problems, I prayed more often, went to church every time the doors were open and even read my Bible looking for answers. As you read in the previous chapter, it was noon in the middle of the week, and it was my problem that pushed me to go to church when I heard from God.

God wants our attention and often has to put us in tough situations so that he can ultimately save us. Salvation is God's way of saying I love you, I forgive you for your sins (Isaiah 43:4). Salvation is when we truly open the door for a relationship with God. Now God's expectation is for us to maintain our relationship by living a holy life by obeying the Ten Commandments (Exodus 20).

Scripture Reading:

Isaiah 12:4

In that day you will say: "Give praise to the Lord, proclaim his name; make known among the nations what he has done, and proclaim that his name is exalted."

Affirmation:

My problems are just part of the process. I will pray until I am through the process. I will trust that God is walking side by side with me. He will never leave me.

What area(s) of your life are under attack? Why do you think this area(s) are being attacked? What is the enemy trying to stop?

Thoughts:

_____
_____
_____
_____
_____
_____
_____
_____
_____
_____
_____

Prayer:

Lord, I seek you today not to ask for anything but to give you all the honor, praise and glory. I thank you for always sending a right on time word. I thank you for the ability to discern the difference between good and evil. You have given me wisdom, knowledge and power. You deserve my unconditional praise not for the many things you have done but simply because you are God Almighty! Amen!

Chapter 10 – The Process

We have to understand God allows situations to happen in your life. These situations help you increase your faith in God. It is all part of a process that will help you fulfill your destiny. In order to handle what God has ordained you for, you must focus on your future. Think of it like goal setting. To get to your goal you may have to take several steps. Writing this book is definitely a testimony of that. I had been writing in my journal for several years before I received the instruction to write a book. My journals served as the first needed step to fulfilling what God wanted me to do. If your mind is fixated on your current situation, you will miss what God is trying to do in the process of resolving your situation. In the book of Job, God allowed Job to be directly tested by Satan. Satan first takes everything that was important to him, his family, his fortune, his possessions, yet continues to be trust and be faithful to God. The second test was Job's health. Satan struck Job with ulcers and scabs from head to toe. Yet, Job said nothing against God. To make things even worst, Job's so-called friends even blamed him for everything that had occurred to him. Of course he must be a sinner if all these bad things had occurred. Right? Absolutely, not! This was all part of God's plan for Job. Through all of his trials and bad advice from his friend's, Job continued to trust God. God was actually growing Job; that is the process. Through Job's story, God helps us understand that we will not always understand what He is doing in our lives, but we should remain humble and faithful. Not only did God restore Job's fortune—he doubled it! You have to go through the process.

Right now your path may seem unclear, your marriage rocky, your children misbehaving, and your bills piling up. Humble yourself. God is still with you. You cannot minister to others if you have not been through something. God can and will look beyond all your perfect imperfections and use you to help someone else in their time of need. He can bring success even when you think you have failed. I charge you to see yourself as God sees you. Your goal is to please God and not worry about what people around you are saying. You are exactly where God wants you to be. Sometime He may intentionally keep you in your situation to ensure you learn at each step of the process. Just because you have not received an answer when expected, it does not mean God will not deliver. Delay does not always mean denied. Wait and do not worry. You are under God's protection. The devil cannot get to you! The devil is only doing what God allows.

I know you are wondering why "it" has not been done. God does not answer all of our prayers immediately or even the way we want Him to. But He uses each step to help us get closer to our destiny. Those who are living an honest and loving life, are covered by His grace and mercy. According to 2 John 1:3, "Grace, mercy, and peace will be with you from God the Father and from the Lord Jesus Christ, the Son of the Father, in truth and love." God wants you to understand everything comes from Him. We have been given the authority to stand against the enemy. Luke 10: 19 says, "Behold, I give you the authority to trample on serpents and scorpions, and over all the power of the enemy, and nothing shall by any means hurt you." Therefore, in the middle of your situation, stand up and tell the devil you can and will not be moved. When he roars, you confuse him by praising God. God can turn the worst thing in your life to the best thing in your life. When you begin to praise Him, pray and believe His word, then it's already done.

Scripture Reading:

Psalm: 34:1-22

I will bless the LORD at all times: his praise shall continually be in my mouth. My soul shall make her boast in the LORD: the humble shall hear thereof, and be glad. O magnify the LORD with me, and let us exalt his name together.

Affirmation:

I understand that God allows situations to happen in my life. These situations will help me increase my faith in him. It is all part of a process that will help me fulfill my destiny and purpose.

What are some things that God may be teaching you in this situation?

Thoughts:

_____

_____

_____

_____

Prayer:

Lord, as you walk with me through this process, I want to remain humble and faithful. I pray to keep my eyes and ears focused on you. I ask you to surround me with people who will encourage and uplift me when my circumstances seem unbearable. Send a word of confirmation when I need a reminder that you are right there with me in the midst of my storm. In Jesus' name, Amen.

Chapter 11 – The Test

The dreaded test. I remember the first time I tried out for the school's basketball team. The gym was full of long-legged girls running up and down the court. I had managed to survive the first two cuts. It was the last day of try outs and I wanted to impress the coach. I was so nervous that my hands trembled almost uncontrollably. I tried to focus on getting the ball in the ring but seemed to miss every time. I knew I had practiced to the best of my ability but still did not make the team. The same thing happens in your spiritual life. Expect your faith to be tested over and over again. The Bible has several scriptures that tell us we will be tested. Psalm 66:10, "For you, God, tested us; you refined us like silver." As can see the test resulted in a change, a promotion to a new level in your relationship with Him. While you are going through your test or other words trials and tribulations you must maintain an attitude of joy. James 1:12 reads, "Blessed is the one who perseveres under trial because, having stood the test, that person will receive the crown of life that the Lord has promised."

There are four different tests you will encounter on your journey. The first test is the situational test. You have been placed in your specific situation now to prove your faith. Do you trust God? Even though you may not be able to understand why you are going through this situation, just praise God and keep believing in him. The second test is called the self-test. The self-test is a test where you must examine your situation for yourself to prove things based on the word of God. Pause here for a moment and think about your situation, where do you see God? Look closely, He is there.

Next is the satanic test. Satan will come to bring adversity and confusion to you. He is attempting to get you to back away from the word of God. Do not be afraid. Do not worry. You are fully equipped to handle this situation. It's a fixed fight. Remember God knew this day would come it was purposely designed for you. That means you will be victorious. Go ahead and declare yourself a winner. The fight is easy simply use the word of God to speak to your situation.

And lastly, there is the sovereign test. During this test, God allows situations to happen so you can trust Him. This test can be difficult because you think God caused this situation to happen. That is not necessarily the case; God may have allowed it to happen so you can increase your faith in Him. Often during this test you will not understand it, but must remain faithful and trust God. The challenge will be beyond your comfort zone. How else could he get your attention if you didn't need someone greater than yourself or man?

Now that you know you will be tested, it is time to discuss how to pass it. The first step in passing the test is to saturate yourself in the Word. In the parable of the sower, Jesus says, "Whoever has ears to hear, let them hear." God is always willing to speak to each of us and give us understanding of His word. There are those who are willing to hear and those whose mind is yet not opened to hear from God. It's obvious if you are still reading this chapter you are anxious to hear more about passing the test.

The next step that will bring you closer to passing your test is to sanctify your thought life. Sanctify means to make holy, or purify. How do you purify your thoughts? Keep your mind on God, not your situation. In addition to keeping your mind stayed on God, also consider the people you spend the most time with. Who are your friends and how well can you depend on them for godly counsel? When you are trying to find your way, this is not the time for the blind to be leading the blind. Your prayer warriors need to be able to guide and mentor you. Their strong relationships with God will serve to encourage you, as will their testimonies of how they overcame by the grace of God. The Bible tells us in Proverbs 27:17, "As iron sharpens iron, so a man sharpens the countenance of his friend."

As I mentioned before, focus on God's promise, not your problem. Remember you are going THROUGH; you have not arrived at your final destination. The test has a time limit. A loss of focus can prolong the length of your test and delay your blessing. Continue to pray and focus on the promise to help you pass the test.

And lastly, remember there is power in the tongue. Proverbs 18:21 states, "Death and life are in the power of the tongue, and those who love it will eat its fruit." As I mentioned before, you have the ability to speak for and against your situation. We have been given the power to manipulate our situation. I had an aunt who was in constant prayer over her son's lives. Her prayer was simply that she would rather see them in jail than dead. God answered her prayers. Both sons maintained a life of drugs and crimes and did not die. Can you guess where they are today? Jail. She did not realize she was speaking jail into their destiny. Her prayer should have been more purposeful maybe asking for her sons to turn away from a life of crime and become youth advocates or community leaders. Speak in agreement with God's Word, His purpose. Continue to remind Him and yourself that the victory is yours in every situation and every test you will encounter.

Scripture Reading:

John 14:1

"Do not let your hearts be troubled. You believe in God; believe also in me."

Affirmation:

This is only a test. There are four different tests that I may encounter during my journey – situational, self-test, satanic test, sovereign. The situational test is a test in a specific situation to prove my faith. The self-test is where I would prove to myself based on the Word of God. The satanic test is designed to confuse me and cause me to back away from God. The sovereign test allows God to use situations to happen so I can trust solely Him.

Thoughts:

What type of test are you currently in? Describe your test. What steps will you take to ensure you pass the test?

_____
_____
_____
_____
_____
_____
_____
_____
_____
_____
_____
_____
_____
_____

_____

_____

_____

_____

_____

Prayer:

Heavenly Father, I thank you for the tests I may encounter. Thank you for the problems, and I thank you even more for the promise of victory. I declare and decree victory today, in your son Jesus' name. No matter what the test may be, I will remain faithful knowing you have designed this test just for me and I am fully equipped to handle this situation. Amen.

Chapter 12 – The Anointing

After you have passed the test, comes the anointing. Everyone is anointed, or called, by God to do something. To clarify, this should not be confused with the idea of a minister anointing a person with oil. Oil is used as a symbol for the presence of the Holy Spirit. People are anointed by God to signify His blessing or call on their life. A person is anointed for a special purpose designed specifically for them. Only God can anoint a person. Only he can stir something up inside you that you will not be able to explain. He is about to give you power unlike any you have ever experienced before. That power is your anointing. In order to release your anointing, you must be obedient to what God instructs you to do.

In the book of Exodus, Moses is called to lead the Jews out of Egypt. He questions God's wisdom in choosing him for this task. How was he supposed to carry out God's Will? What was he to say? God not only gave him instructions on what to do, He assured Moses that He would be with him every step of the way. As he ventured on this journey, God provided signs that He was with him every step of the way to the Promised Land. During the day, there were pillars of clouds and at night pillars of fire army. Today's pillars may not be made of clouds or fire, but God still guides us daily.

When I came to understand that God was calling me to be an evangelist, I was nervous and excited all in once. I didn't really understand what it meant to be called an evangelist and had to do research to understand what it truly meant. I have learned that we can get so focused on titles that we miss the point. As of today, I have not officially received a title but I am certain God has given me an assignment. At this time, it was simply to tell my story. He first instructed me to be interesting. Now that's funny.

When I first began to journal about my life, it was more painful to me than interesting. As years have gone by, and I have re-read them over and over and there truly were a few "interesting" things that happened in my life to help me become the person I am today. My goal is simply to be warm and genuine and tell how God has been a part of every aspect of my life in hopes that I can help you become closer to Him.

God is calling you. He first called you into your body, in other words your birthdate. Then he called you in the body of Christ. Ephesians 4:4 reads, "There is one body and one

Spirit, just as you were called in one hope of your calling." During this time of your life, as you begin to understand your calling, you will gain some things. You will lose the fascination with people who are only fascinated with your body. You will attract those people who are fall in love with your spirit. The closer you walk with Jesus, you will lose your old self and walk into who you really ae. You are walking into your purpose. You must continue to think highly of yourself, believe that your calling is important. Enjoy where you are at this moment, each level is perfectly designed for you. Learn the lesson and be prepared for your assignment.

Once you accept your assignment, things will fall into place. Success is a product of what you think. Start to think it and speak it. Get control of your life by controlling your thoughts. You can do all things. So stop feeling sorry for yourself and look into the mirror and say, "I am a child of God." Remember where God has brought you from, it's your story. Don't forget where you came from. It is part of who you are and shaping you into who you are destined to be. YOU were called, but your journey will not be easy.

Paul submitted his life to God and trusted Him. He faced insults, rejection and many difficult situations. So let me be clear, so will you. You will be faced with opposition and attacks from the enemy. Put on your whole armor of God and know that you are victorious. When you are working for the Lord, expect to get haters. Haters are your enemies that came out of the closet, they want what you have but they don't even understand what you went through it get it. Don't waste your time trying to figure out why they are hating on you. Just know that God will prepare a table before your enemies (Psalm 23:5). Haters try to keep up with what God is doing in your life. They often criticize and try their best to derail your destiny, your purpose. When this happens, you have to learn to encourage yourself. Tell yourself, I will survive. Learn to love yourself. Take hate and change it into motivation. Use whatever they say as a launching pad to push you further into your calling. If you have problems in your life, keep it moving. If God has called you, he is already aware of all you will encounter. He will continue to move you in the right direction. The best in you will show up when your back is up against the wall. The greater your opposition, the greater your calling.

Scripture Reading

2 Corinthians 1:21-22

Now he which stablisheth us with you in Christ, and hath anointed us, is God; who hath also sealed us, and given the earnest of the Spirit in our hearts.

Romans 8:29-30

For whom he did foreknow, he also did predestinate to be conformed to the image of his Son, that he might be the firstborn among many brethren. Moreover whom he did predestinate, them he also called: and whom he called, them he also justified: and whom he justified, them he also glorified.

Affirmation:

I was born with a specific purpose in mind. I will be obedient and do what I have been called to do. I will graciously accept my purpose in life. Today, I will take the next step in becoming the woman God called me to become.

Thoughts:

What things do you love to do? What excites you? What keeps you up at night? What comes to you naturally?

_____
_____
_____
_____
_____
_____
_____
_____
_____
_____
_____
_____
_____
_____
_____
_____
_____
_____
_____
_____

What obstacles are stopping you from doing those things? How will you overcome them?

Prayer:

Lord, thank you for calling me. I am a sinner but I thank you for trusting me with your precious gifts. I am crying out to you. I want less of me and more of you. Release your anointing in me. Allow me to do all that you have called me to do. Thank you for the light you have instilled in me. I ask that you continue to increase my confidence and faith. I will do all that you ask of me. Allow your message to be forwarded through me, not to stop within. As I continue to grow and fulfill your purpose for my life, send me clear instructions. Allow me to clearly discern those who are for me and those you will use to bless me. Continue to use me and I will give you all the honor, praise and glory. In Jesus' name, Amen!

Chapter 13 – Break Every Chain

Generational curses are mentioned in the Bible as a warning given to Jews that they should worship *only* God. If a generation did not honor that command and worshipped anything other than God, the next generation would be punished for the sins of their fathers. In the Old Testament, the effects of sin were passed down from one generation to the next. You have to break the cycle of those things that were brought down thru your bloodline. God has given you the authority to change your life. When God wants to change a family, He changes one person. In case you haven't figured it out yet, that's you. As a child of God, the transfer of generational curses have stopped with you.

You may find yourself wondering whether or not your family is bound by a generational curse. Symptoms of a generational curse are easily identified from one generation to the next. There will be a pattern of negative behavior present in every gencration. Some examples include:

- Is there constant failure? Depression?
- Is there high level of uncontrollable rage or anger?

- Is there a history of alcohol, physical, sexual or substance abuse?
- Is there a history of family illnesses? Cancer? High blood pressure?
- Is there a history of financial difficulties?

Now that you are able to recognize generational curses, it is time to break those chains.

First you must begin by identifying your family's curse. You cannot be delivered from a problem you are not willing to admit you have. Next, pray with scriptures to align your words with the will of God and generational chains will be broken. Release your negative thoughts, attitudes, and words and replace them with positive thoughts, and actions. Recognize the enemy and realize the battle is not yours alone.

And finally, you must continue to follow the instructions. God has given us commandments to live by but he also speaks to us through prayer, praise, reading His word, song, or even through others. Be obedient and do as you are instructed. Sometimes this will be easy but I would be lying to you if I said that's always the case.

Writing this book is the perfect example of being obedient. I never desired to write a book before, but God made it clear this is what He wanted me to do. He gave me a foundation through years of keeping a journal. As I began working on the manuscript, He would wake me up throughout the night, laying specific scriptures on my heart to read and to make note of. It was unclear to what the scriptures meant to me but I kept reading and asking God to make the instructions clear. And He did.

You have the instructions now break the curse and accept the blessing. Luke 11:28 teaches us that blessings come from hearing God and doing what you are instructed to do. The fantastic thing about God is not only will He bless you for your obedience, but your family, and your community.

Scripture Reading:

Exodus 20:4-6

"You shall not make for yourself a carved image—any likeness of anything that is in heaven above, or that is in the earth beneath, or that is in the water under the earth; you shall not bow down to them nor serve them. For I, the LORD your

God, am a jealous God, visiting the iniquity of the fathers upon the children to the third and fourth generations of those who hate Me, but showing mercy to thousands, to those who love Me and keep My commandments."

Matthew 5: 6

"Blessed are those who hunger and thirst for righteousness, for they will be filled."

Affirmation: I am blessed. My marriage is blessed. My children are blessed. My family is blessed. My job is blessed. My finances are blessed. Every generational curse has been broken in my life. God has promised me generations of blessings.

Thoughts:

What generational curses have plagued you or your family?

_____
_____
_____
_____

Find a scripture that speaks to this curse. Write out a prayer that aligns the scripture to your situation. Then replace every word you say and thought that enters your mind with something positive.

_____

_____

Prayer:

Lord, forgive me for all of my sins. I repent. God cleanse me. Release anything or anyone in my life and my family's life that hold us in spiritual bondage. I replace them with love, prosperity, joy, peace, and forgiveness. I recognize the enemy and speak against addiction, financial constraints, hurt, depression, anger and everything negative in our lives. I break every curse that has held my family in bondage for the past four generations. I declare and decree my family is blessed. My children's children are free, saved and blessed. It is a new beginning. For me and my house we will serve the Lord. In Jesus' name, Amen!

Chapter 14 – Power

In the previous chapter we talked about breaking chains but you can't do it by yourself. Hopefully, I didn't mislead you but you need POWER. You need God's help in all that you do. Power is an inherent characteristic of God. Power is the Holy Spirit inside. Romans 8:11, "But if the Spirit of Him who raised Jesus from the dead dwells in you, He who raised Christ from the dead will also give life to your mortal bodies through His Spirit who dwells in you." Power simply put is a source of our means. I won't get into a deep meaning of the Holy Spirit but I want you to understand it's the guiding principle that gives you the power or authority to act. Second Peter 1:3-5 confirms the power inside you, "His divine power has given to us all things that pertain to life and godliness, through the knowledge of Him who called us by glory and virtue, for by which have been given to us exceedingly great and precious promises, that through these you may be partakers of the divine nature, having escaped the corruption that is in the world through lust." I want to focus on how to find and use the power inside of you.

To obtain this power you must first die to yourself. What I must die? Well, not exactly. According to Romans 6:11-14, "Likewise you also, reckon yourselves to be dead indeed to sin, but alive to God in Christ Jesus our Lord. Therefore, do not let sin reign in your mortal body, that you should obey it in its lusts. And do not present your members as instruments of unrighteousness to sin, but present yourselves to God as being alive from the dead, and your members as instruments of righteousness to God. For sin shall not have dominion over you, for you are not under law but under grace." God will not flow through unclean vessels; therefore you must repent of your sins and wrong doings, ask for forgiveness and consistently pray. During this time of cleansing and renewal, God will often put you in isolation. He will separate you from your friends and even family. Any and everything to get your attention focused on Him. Isolation can be a very lonely place at times but remember its part of the process of creating a new powerful you. He has put you in a place to feed upon His word. Even though you may feel lonely, you are not alone. God's presence will be with you. Jeremiah 29:13, "And you will seek Me and find Me, when you search for Me with all your heart." Read your Bible, and pray. The things that have been unclear in your life will begin to become clearer. You will gain a stronger understanding of who you are. You are powerful. Now, that you understand your power, let's talk about what you can do with it.

The words you speak have power. God spoke the world into being by the power of His words (Psalm 33:9). Words can either agree with heaven or hell. They can bless or curse. The writer of Proverbs 18:21 tells us, "The tongue has the power of life and death, and those who love it will eat its fruit." Words can lift people up or destroy their spirit and we will have to take into account on the Day of Judgment for every word we have spoken. Activate your power by using words to bring upon desired change. You have the power to speak life into your situation. Simply speak positive affirmations daily. I set out to tackle all the problems in my life by speaking God's Word over and over again. I will be the lender and not the borrower. My child is saved. My marriage is saved. I will forgive those who have hurt me. I will be a positive example to all I encounter. These words were a true representation of my heart and I wanted to bombard God with constant reminders of what I was praying for.

Don't just speak the words but think it and believe it. As we are reminded in Matthew 21:22, "And whatever you ask in prayer, you will receive, if you have faith." If you can think, you can change, you can evolve, you can move. Your thoughts can often be the problem. You are just one thought away from the greatest experience that you may have in your life. Your thoughts have the power to bring you up or down. When I relocated for my new job, I moved to a new city almost two hundred miles from home and my family. I had a lot of time to myself and was lonely. Then I decided to look at my situation in a different way. There were so many benefits to being alone. I had nothing but time to read and study and prepare for this book. Then I took it a step further; my family did not relocate immediately with me and that meant no cooking! I was able to enjoy doing what I wanted even though I was alone. I used my power to change my mind by looking at my situation in a positive manner. I made a conscientious decision to focus on the positive aspects of being alone.

Stop and think about it for a moment. Other people's thoughts have no direct bearing on you. If you make a choice to change your mind then you change your situation. Instead of looking at your situation in a negative way, find the positive. You have the power. Use it.

Scripture Reading:

2 Timothy 1:7-8

For God hath not given us the spirit of fear; but of power, and of love, and of a sound mind. Be not thou therefore ashamed of the testimony of our Lord, nor of me his prisoner: but be thou partaker of the afflictions of the gospel according to the power of God...

Affirmation:

The words I speak have POWER. I have the power to speak life into my situation. I will speak positive affirmations daily. I will tackle every problem in my life by speaking God's Word over and over again.

Affirmations are constant reminders of who you are, who you want to be or a specific outcome you desire. Positive affirmations fight against negative thinking and help you maintain a positive outlook.

List out as many positive affirmations as you can. I am... I will...

Thoughts:

Prayer:

Lord thank you for the power of words and thoughts. Fill me up with YOUR WORD so I can have the right words to say. Give me strength. Give me faith. Thank you for the power to change my situation, to break every chain that has been passed from generation to generation. I speak life into every dead area of my life—spiritual, physical and financial. In Jesus' name, Amen!

Chapter 15 – The Turnaround

I have provided you instructions on how to get a closer relationship with God. You know how to pray. You know how and when to fast. You know that you have to wait. You know you will be tested. You know you have the power to speak into your situation. You know you can break chains. And now it's time for the turnaround. The turnaround is both physical and spiritual. The turnaround is you.

After about ten months in Augusta, we decided to purchase a home. We had become comfortable with the area and knew where we wanted to purchase. I asked God for approval to purchase our home and to deny our loan and make it difficult if this was outside of what He wanted for us. It was Sunday night at 10PM and I went online and applied for a loan. The next morning my phone rang at 8am and by noon everything was approved. Our mortgage payments were almost exactly the same as renting with no money down. We quickly found a house that had everything we wanted and then some. Our closing process went seamlessly. It was perfect. Now, that God had blessed us with our home, I wanted to give Him thanks.

About a month later, I was sitting in my office talking to another manager when I heard God say ask her to have her Pastor bless our home. She said she was certain he would and would get back to me. He agreed and scheduled to come out later that week. When he and his wife arrived, they had such a warm welcoming presence. I was very comfortable with inviting them into our home. My husband and I introduced ourselves and we gave them a quick tour. The pastor announced that it was time to pray and bless our home. We prayed and blessed the house to the Lord. It was much more than I expected. The pastor had my husband recite various prayers to bless the entire house, including the doors, the windows, the pictures, and even the furniture. He then motioned for my husband to stand facing the front window as he prayed. It was a powerful moment watching him as he gazed out the window, praying and committing himself to being the head of our household, protector, father, and husband. It warmed my heart.

We finished the ceremony and the pastor's wife asked if it was ok for her to pray for us. We formed a circle, joined hands and she began to lead us in pray. She proclaimed that the Holy Spirit said this was our year of restoration. She said we needed to leave everything that happened in Charleston behind us. How did she know we had turmoil in Charleston? She informed us that God was restoring our marriage and we needed it. She said it was time for both of us to step into our purpose. She told my husband if he wanted a new business that all he had to do was ask God for it. The pastor interjected saying when my husband stepped up and prayed God would open up all of our blessings. He said that he also had the power to declare and decree to bind up any trap that the enemy had set before us. This prayer aligned up to exactly what was going on in our lives. I was so emotional because of recent events and this was my reminder that God had heard my cries and once again confirming His presence. Our turnaround had actually occurred when we relocated.

During that time my son decided that he would not be returning to college after his first year and that he would be returning home for a year to save money. My husband and I were devastated at first at the news. We could not believe he was throwing away a full academic scholarship to sit at home and work a minimum wage job. This was not part of our plan that we had for his life. However, we supported his decision and gave him gas money to drive himself from New Orleans to Charleston. If it wasn't our plan, we weren't going to necessarily make things super easy either. He decided that he preferred to stay with his grandmother than return to our home in Augusta. I was disappointed to say the least but understood it was not my decision.

I continued to pray and remind God that He said my son would be the first male in several generations to graduate college. The summer went by and he worked odd jobs here and there. He encountered a few situations that truly tested my faith but God continued to keep His hands around him. The seasons changed and so did he. My son actually had become very intrigued with eating healthier to maintain a better lifestyle. His grandmother was suffering from Stage 4 bone cancer and he created a diet focused on fighting cancer and increasing her energy. He helped her daily with taking all her medications as prescribed. Her energy increased and she began to return to her normal activities. She even began to cook which she had not done in quite some time. His presence around her was exactly what she needed, a turn around.

He began to read the Bible and Koran and compare and contrast with his African American studies. I thought to myself did that historically black college change him into a Muslim. Again, that wasn't the plan that I had for his life. Then I read that all great scholars studied several different religions and that helped ease my tension. As the holidays approached, he decided he was ready to return to school and that he wanted to relocate with us. I was both surprised and excited. He had actually saved enough money to move into his own place with a roommate. He returned to school the following semester. This time he was different.

He had made a decision and choice that he would turn his life around. His first semester he focused on his academic studies and working. We saw him very little to say we lived in the same city less than 10 miles apart. He continued to push academically and ended his first semester with extraordinary results. I realized that the time away from school allowed him to find himself and focus on things that were more important. He had also had a turn around.

Scripture Reading:

Romans 8:28

"And we know that in all things God works for the good of those who love him, who have been called according to his purpose."

Affirmation:

I know how to pray. I know how to fast. I am patient in waiting, I will be tested. I have the power to speak into any situation. And now it is time for a turnaround to manifest.

How do you think your story could impact the lives of others? Who will you share your personal story with? When will you share?

Thoughts:

_____
_____
_____
_____
_____

Prayer:

Lord, I thank you for this season of my turnaround. I pray you increase my knowledge and understanding of my situation.

Allow me to see that all things have a purpose even when I cannot understand them. I declare and decree I will be the lender and not the borrower. My family is saved. My faith, desire, and commitment to do everything you ask is increased. In Jesus' name, Amen.

Chapter 16 – Praise and Worship

As you step into your calling praise and worship will be your weapons to fight every battle. Worship is simply to glorify, honor, exalt, and please God (Psalm 145:3). Worship is our time to reflect on how great God has been in our lives even during those times when we may have not always said or done the right thing. Praise is more of an act of worship. They both go hand in hand. Worship brings us closer to God. Any many people worship God in different ways. Jesus told the woman at the well, in John 4:24, that those who wish to worship God MUST do so in spirit and in truth. We need to go to the creator with the right attitude and for the right reasons. We can worship God through praise, song, prayer and even dance. Some worship is done in private and often can be seen done publicly. Remember, it's personal, it's your relationship and you decide when and how you will worship and praise God. We often get them confused. Praise is thanking God for all he has done for us. To praise God is to honor Him. If you need God to rest inside you, then you need to open your mouth. You have to give Him a place to live. Everywhere you go He is with you; during good times and bad. When you open up and praise God you open up the doors to your victory in your situation. You don't have to fight. He will have your enemies fight themselves. Instead of being depressed and caught up in your situation praise God. Praise Him in advance for your breakthrough. Praise keeps your dreams alive; its faith in action. It only takes one praise to shift the atmosphere. Praise God right now!

Exactly how do I praise Him? There are a few ways if you are not quite sure how to praise Him. There are seven Hebrews words for *praise* described in the Old Testament. I have listed several scriptures to reference. Keep in mind that the Bible was originally written in Hebrew and later translated to English. Therefore, you will see the word praise in the text and not the Hebrew word listed below.

- **Yadah:** This is worship with your hands raised up receiving from the Lord (Genesis 29:35).
- **Towdah:** This is where we offer the sacrifice of praise as we stand in faith, even when it looks like the promises of God are not working (Psalm 42:4-5).
- **Halal:** This where you use your whole body to celebrate by worshipping and praising God (1 Chronicles 16:4).

- **Barak:** This is worship where you kneel to bless God as an act of adoration and to bless God expecting to receive something (Psalm 103).
- **Shabach:** Shouting your praise with a loud voice will call your spirit to attention, and hinder the hosts of hell (Psalm 117:1).
- **Zamar:** This is worship with all kinds of musical instruments (Psalm 92:1).
- **Tehillah:** This is where you sing songs of praise to the Lord (Psalm 22:3).

However you choose to praise Him—by lifting your hands, with singing, with words, with dancing or even with instruments—it's your personal choice. Worship is praising God for who He is. It requires an invitation from God. And good news, you have been invited. God has personally invited each of us individually. He is always there but you may not always see Him. When we see Him, it's often in the middle of our trials and tribulations. During our periods of brokenness, He will reveal Himself. Worship allows us to enter His presence. You are required to approach Him with a total dependency in the spirit not flesh. Instead of cursing your situation, active your power through your praise and worship and watch God work on your behalf.

Scripture Reading:

Psalm 138:2

"I will worship toward thy holy temple, and praise thy name for thy loving kindness and for thy truth: for thou hast magnified thy word above all thy name."

Affirmation:

Praise and worship are my time to reflect on how great God has been in my life. My worship will bring me closer to God.

Thoughts:

Provide an example of when God did something for you? How did you feel? Who did you tell?

_____
_____
_____
_____
_____

When God answers your prayer this time, how will you praise and worship him?

Prayer:

Lord, I lift my hands to you. I praise and worship you. I am not concerned how others perceive my worship. My sole purpose is to thank you for all you have done, are doing, and will do, and most importantly, just for being who you are, God Almighty. Amen.

Chapter 17 – Miracles, Signs and Wonders

It's time for you to expect a miracle. Miracles are events that occur that are unexplainable by man but ordained by God. First Corinthians 12:28, "And God has appointed these in the church: first apostles, second prophets, third teachers, after that miracles, then gifts of healings, helps, administrations, varieties of tongues." There are many miracles that occurred throughout the Bible. In the Old Testament, there is the story of the three Hebrew boys—Shadrach, Meshach and Abednego—that stood in a fiery furnace unharmed (Daniel 3). Jonah was swallowed by a whale and was vomited up alive three days later (Jonah 1). And even one of my favorites Jesus walked on water (Matthew 14:22-33). I come to tell you today that God is still performing miracles, signs and wonders.

One beautiful sunny Sunday afternoon, I was in my car driving from Charleston to my home in Augusta and I was thinking about my son and all he was going through. I was angry with God. Yes, I said it. I was angry with God. I began to pray and remind God of all the things He had promised me. And I thought I am not settling for anything less than my promise. I told myself my God is a promise keeper. I turned the radio on and tuned into a broadcast from Pastor Joel Osteen. He quickly got my attention. His sermon was on having faith. He was telling a story about a mother who was always praying for her son and he was constantly getting in trouble and ended up in jail; sounded familiar to me. She was hurt and confused and questioned her faith. Yep, he was talking about me. He then said, "Even when you have a little faith, God has big faith." He said to get ready for a divine shift. God is making His way and we should prepare for a bunch of first time favors in your life. I thought to myself, "God is this message for me?" I looked to my left and there was the biggest rainbow I had ever seen in my life. The sky was completely clear and I could see a full rainbow with bright rays all around it. I quickly grabbed my cell phone and snapped a picture. I even tried to video tape it because I needed proof of what just happened. I recommend you do not try to drive and take pictures. I turned to focus on the road and when I glanced again the rainbow was gone as quickly as it had appeared. This was my personal reminder of God's promise to me.

Several months later, I am glad to report my son is doing well. He is currently seeking a degree in anthropology with a minor in economics and is also a business owner. His life experiences have truly molded him into a wonderful young man. He has decided to take another path—one focused on improving his mind, body, and soul. And I am thankful to have him back home.

Miracles serve as a reminder that God is still alive. They cause nonbelievers to believe. Miracles, signs and wonders continue to increase your faith. They may not present as a rainbow, a dream or even in the form of a person anointed by God, but remember this: miracles, signs and wonders are as much a part of today as they were during biblical times. Continue focusing on the tools God has given you. Wake up every day anticipating a miracle. Expect God to be in all things.

Scripture Reading:

Hebrews 2:3-4

"How shall we escape, if we neglect so great salvation; which at the first began to be spoken by the Lord, and was confirmed unto us by them that heard him; God also bearing them witness, both with signs and wonders, and with divers miracles, and gifts of the Holy Ghost, according to his own will?"

Affirmation:

I will expect a miracle every day. God is a promise keeper. Every miracle is a reminder that God is still alive and present in my life.

What miracle have occurred in your life? If God did it then, he can do it AGAIN!

Thoughts:

_____
_____
_____
_____
_____
_____
_____
_____
_____

Prayer:

Lord, I thank you for being in the miracle making business. I expect a miracle today. I thank you for sending me signs and wonders when my faith becomes weary in the wait. I will continue to press forward until my promise has been manifested. In Jesus' name, Amen.

Chapter 18 – It Is Well!

I am confident to begin this chapter by saying, "It is well!" My journey has allowed me to enter a place of thanksgiving and peace with whatever is set before me. Even when God says "No," I give him honor and praise. God has purposely placed me in several different tests to help me get to this place called peace. Today I can proudly write that I closely hold on to God's promises. Regardless of what the situation looks like, God either did it or allowed it. I find silly little things, like marbles that were given to me by a Pastor during a prayer meeting that I hold on to as constant reminders that God made me a promise and I could always remind him of such. Through constant fasting, praying and praise I am still making it through. I use the power of words to encourage and uplift me and all that I encounter.

So today, I encourage you to do the same. He promised that the generational curses of addiction that have bestowed my family are broken. God has promised me that my son would be a leader of many at a young age. God promised me financial prosperity and a covenant marriage. I have learned… IT IS WELL!

Scripture Reading:

Jeremiah 29:11

"For I know the plans I have for you," declares the LORD, "plans to prosper you and not to harm you, plans to give you hope and a future."

Affirmation:

My journey has allowed me to enter a place of thanksgiving and peace for whatever is set before me. I will give God honor and praise. I will be who God has called me to be. I am fully equipped. I am made in his image. I am perfect. I am loved. I have a purpose in life. I will spend the rest of my life being me.

Thoughts:

What actions will you take now that you have completed this book? What are you goals for this year? How will you know when you are successful?

_____

_____

Prayer:

Heavenly Father, I thank you for the knowledge you have bestowed upon me. I thank you for trusting me to do your work. I thank you for your power and your anointing. Today, I will continue this unknown journey trusting and knowing you are my guide. I will continue to seek your face and do all you ask of me. I trust you, knowing no matter what my eyes may see or ears may hear, IT IS WELL! Amen! Amen! Amen!

Acknowledgments

*Writing **It Is Well!** was not an easy task and I am deeply humbled that God chose me to simply tell my story. Thank God for trusting me. I am thankful for my tribe for their constant love and support. I am blessed to be surrounded by several amazing women that love me in all of my imperfect ways. I am proud of the woman I am today because I went through one hell of a time becoming her.*

Unapologetically,

Shana

Biography

Biography

Shana Anderson is a wife, mother, author, mentor, coach and inspirational leader. In 2019, she became an ordained minister, which she regards as her most prized accomplishment. A graduate of Southern Wesleyan University in 2005, she holds a Bachelor of Science in Business Management. In 2017, Shana obtained a Master of Business Administration - Project Management from Ashford University. She authored an inspirational book, "It Is Well" based on her life experiences and personal relationship with God. She created a women in business forum called Girl Talk which focuses on empowering and developing women in leadership roles. Shana is currently the Chief Operating Officer of Choose Synergy, a coaching and business consulting company dedicated to helping companies and individuals reach their maximum potential and purpose.

Stay connected:

ShanaWilsonAnderson.com

Made in the USA
Middletown, DE
22 November 2025